MW01227671

Computer users are not all alike.
Neither are SYBEX books.

We know our customers have a variety of needs. They've told us so. And because we've listened, we've developed several distinct types of books to meet the needs of each of our customers. What are you looking for in computer help?

If you're looking for the basics, try the **ABC's** series, or for a more visual approach, select **Teach Yourself.**

Mastering and **Understanding** titles offer you a step-by-step introduction, plus an in-depth examination of intermediate-level features, to use as you progress.

Our **Up & Running** series is designed for computer-literate consumers who want a no-nonsense overview of new programs. Just 20 basic lessons, and you're on your way.

SYBEX **Encyclopedias** and **Desktop References** provide a comprehensive reference and explanation of all of the commands, features and functions of the subject software.

Sometimes a subject requires a special treatment that our standard series don't provide. So you'll find we have titles like **Advanced Techniques, Handbooks, Tips & Tricks,** and others that are specifically tailored to satisfy a unique need.

You'll find SYBEX publishes a variety of books on every popular software package. Looking for computer help? Help Yourself to SYBEX.

For a complete catalog of our publications:

SYBEX Inc.
2021 Challenger Drive, Alameda, CA 94501
Tel: (510) 523-8233/(800) 227-2346 Telex: 336311
Fax: (510) 523-2373

Look for the *Up & Running* books on a variety of popular software and hardware topics. Current titles include:

AutoSketch 3

Carbon Copy Plus

Clipper 5.01

CorelDRAW 2

dBASE III PLUS

DOS 3.3

DOS 5

DR DOS 5.0

Excel 3 for Windows

Flight Simulator

Grammatik IV 2.0

Harvard Graphics

Harvard Graphics 3

Lotus 1-2-3 Release 2.2

Louts 1-2-3 for Windows

Lotus 1-2-3 Release 2.3

Lotus 1-2-3 Release 3.1

Mac Classic

Macintosh System 7

Norton Desktop for Windows

Norton Utilities 5

Norton Utilities on the Macintosh

PageMaker 4 on the PC

PageMaker on the Macintosh

PC Tools Deluxe 6

PROCOMM PLUS

PROCOMM PLUS 2.0

Q & A

Q & A 4

Quattro Pro 3

Quicken 4

ToolBook for Windows

Windows 3.0

Windows 286/386

Word for Windows

WordPerfect 5.1

WordPerfect for Windows

WordPerfect Library/Office PC

XTreeGold 2

Up & Running
with CompuServe®

Bob Campbell

SYBEX®

San Francisco • Paris • Düsseldorf • Soest

Acquisitions Editor: Dianne King
Series Editor: Joanne Cuthbertson
Editor: David Krassner
Technical Editor: Michael Warren
Word Processors: Ann Dunn and Susan Trybull
Book Designer: Elke Hermanowski
Icon Designer: Helen Bruno
Screen Graphics: Coung Le
Desktop Production Artist: Helen Bruno
Proofreaders: Arno Lockheart Harris and David Avilla Silva
Indexer: Julie Kawabata
Cover Designer: Archer Design

Screen reproductions produced by XenoFont.

XenoFont is a trademark of XenoSoft.

SYBEX is a registered trademark of SYBEX, Inc.

TRADEMARKS: SYBEX has attempted throughout this book to distinguish proprietary trademarks from descriptive terms by following the capitalization style used by the manufacturer.

SYBEX is not affiliated with any manufacturer.

Every effort has been made to supply complete and accurate information. However, SYBEX assumes no responsibility for its use, nor for any infringement of the intellectual property rights of third parties which would result from such use.

Copyright ©1992 SYBEX Inc., 2021 Challenger Drive, Alameda, CA 94501. World rights reserved. No part of this publication may be stored in a retrieval system, transmitted, or reproduced in any way, including but not limited to photocopy, photograph, magnetic or other record, without the prior agreement and written permission of the publisher.

Library of Congress Card Number: 91-66423
ISBN: 0-7821-1033-9

Manufactured in the United States of America
10 9 8 7 6 5 4 3 2

SYBEX
Up & Running Books

The Up & Running series of books from SYBEX has been developed for committed, eager PC users who would like to become familiar with a wide variety of programs and operations as quickly as possible. We assume that you are comfortable with your PC and that you know the basic functions of word processing, spreadsheets, and database management. With this background, Up & Running books will show you in 20 steps what particular products can do and how to use them.

Who this book is for

Up & Running books are designed to save you time and money. First, you can avoid purchase mistakes by previewing products before you buy them—exploring their features, strengths, and limitations. Second, once you decide to purchase a product, you can learn its basics quickly by following the 20 steps—even if you are a beginner.

What this book provides

The first step usually covers software installation in relation to hardware requirements. You'll learn whether the program can operate with your available hardware as well as various methods for starting the program. The second step often introduces the program's user interface. The remaining 18 steps demonstrate the program's basic functions, using examples and short descriptions.

Contents and structure

A clock shows the amount of time you can expect to spend at your computer for each step. Naturally, you'll need much less time if you only read through the step rather than complete it at your computer.

Special symbols and notes

You can also focus on particular points by scanning the short notes in the margins and locating the sections you are most interested in.

In addition, three symbols highlight particular sections of text:

The Action symbol highlights important steps that you will carry out.

The Tip symbol indicates a practical hint or special technique.

The Warning symbol alerts you to a potential problem and suggestions for avoiding it.

We have structured the Up & Running books so that the busy user spends little time studying documentation and is not burdened with unnecessary text. An Up & Running book cannot, of course, replace a lengthier book that contains advanced applications. However, you will get the information you need to put the program to practical use and to learn its basic functions in the shortest possible time.

We welcome your comments

SYBEX is very interested in your reactions to the Up & Running series. Your opinions and suggestions will help all of our readers, including yourself. Please send your comments to: SYBEX Editorial Department, 2021 Challenger Drive, Alameda, CA 94501.

Preface

CompuServe, now more than twelve years old, has grown into today's premier information utility, with the largest number of services and the widest subscriber base of any public-access network. It combines a solid electronic-mail system with forums on a wide range of topics, hundreds of databases, business and financial services, news services, and more. Nonetheless, CompuServe remains surprisingly accessible and inexpensive.

Up & Running with CompuServe is a tutorial, stressing hands-on use of CompuServe and allowing you to grow comfortable as you explore the service's major features. Specifically, you will learn how to:

- Use CompuServe forums (bulletin boards organized around specific topics). You will learn to exchange messages with other users, conduct conferences, and obtain computer files of all kinds.

- Exchange e-mail messages with other CompuServe subscribers and other e-mail systems.

- Obtain business and financial information, current news, and weather reports.

- Conduct research online with CompuServe's extensive set of databases.

- Find flight information in the Official Airline Guide.

- Automate your CompuServe sessions to find the most information in the shortest time.

The examples are quick and inexpensive. Although the book is primarily tutorial, it does give a solid overview of CompuServe.

To use CompuServe, you need nothing more than a PC, a modem, and a communications program. This book is not a guide to communications programs, but it does offer some pointers. In the first step, you will learn how to obtain an inexpensive communications program to make fullest use of CompuServe. (For a systematic introduction to another communications program, see my *Up & Running with PROCOMM PLUS 2.0*—SYBEX, 1991). *Up & Running with CompuServe* uses the IBM-standard PC in its examples, but offers tips on finding software for the Macintosh and other platforms.

This book uses a few simple conventions. When you are instructed to press Enter, strike the key marked *Return, Enter,* or ↵ on your keyboard. This key is referred to as *<CR>* on CompuServe itself. Command input appears in boldface; for instance, to type **G**, just press *G* without using the shift key. "Enter **go mail**" is shorthand for "type **go mail** and press Enter."

Also, each step is timed to suggest how much time you must actively spend on its exercises. These estimates do *not* include file transfers in the steps, because file-transfer time depends on the speed of your communications link. Finally, when instructed to "turn on logging," this means to turn on the logging feature of your communications program.

Try these simple steps, and you will see that CompuServe is readily accessible, but with enough diversity to hold your interest for a long time.

Bob Campbell
December 1991

Table of Contents

Step 1

Getting Started

CompuServe is so easy to use that you will be making discoveries and doing work almost at once. In this step, you will learn how to become a CompuServe member, how to subscribe to the service, and how to log on and off.

Getting the Basic Ingredients

You will need a few basic elements to become a CompuServe member:

- A personal computer with a modem and a general-purpose communications program
- CompuServe introductory subscription information
- A local CompuServe telephone number

Let's look at these in detail.

Your Computer Hardware and Software

Any computer equipped for connection to remote services can connect you to CompuServe.

Similarly, most communications programs will connect you to CompuServe. To make best use of the service, your program should provide these features:

Your communications program

- A dialing directory for automatic dialing.
- A log file, to keep a record of sessions. (A *log* is a transcript of your "conversations" with CompuServe.)
- File-transfer methods (protocols) designed for use over public networks, such as the CompuServe B protocol or YMODEM, as well as means for ASCII text transfers. *Protocols* are sets of technical procedures for file transfer.

- Means to run other programs without terminating the communications program. This is useful for viewing graphics online, for instance.

- A learn mode to record your frequent interactions with the system (such as logging on) as sequences of prompts and commands called *scripts,* which you can replay to carry out sequences automatically.

If you want to follow the step-by-step examples in this book exactly, you must obtain the shareware program that is used. This inexpensive program is called TELIX and is available by mail or online.

Obtaining   If you don't yet have a communications program, you can call or
TELIX   write the makers of TELIX for information:

Exis Inc.
P.O. Box 130
West Hill ON
Canada M1E 4R4
(416) 289-4641

If you have means to log on to CompuServe initially but would like TELIX anyway, Step 3 details how to download the program directly from CompuServe.

As we go along, I will alert you to more specialized programs to help you in your work with CompuServe. In all cases, these programs can be ordered or downloaded from CompuServe directly.

CompuServe Subscription Information

CompuServe introductory subscriptions come in the form of membership kits, which are available from computer stores or bookstores or by calling the phone number given below. Introductory offers are often supplied as free bonuses with many communications packages, such as PROCOMM PLUS. This material includes sign-up information as well as credits for free time online to explore the system.

Finding Your Local Telephone Number

CompuServe offers a toll-free number for customer service and information on local telephone numbers, basic rates, and log-on instructions. As of this writing, that number is

(800) 635-6225

Dial this number from a touchtone telephone and follow the instructions to get your local CompuServe number. When prompted, dial in your area code and number. You must also provide your modem's communications rate. You can also make choices to receive basic rate information, as well as log-on instructions to reach CompuServe from different public networks.

Understanding Communications Rates

Also called the *baud rate,* the communications rate is the speed at which data are exchanged between your PC and a remote system. CompuServe commonly offers connections at rates of 1200 bits-per-second (*bps* or *baud*), 2400 bps, and 9600 bps. Connect at the highest rate possible, but see the note on communications surcharges below.

Understanding CompuServe Charges

You can learn about basic CompuServe charges through the toll-free telephone number or online (as described in the next step). Here are the basic charges:

- The membership support fee is a fixed subscription charge. It is currently $2.00 per month.

- The Executive Option is a monthly premium that allows access to services of special interest to businesspeople. It is currently $10.00. You can specify this option when you sign up. You can add or remove this service at any time.

- When you are connected to CompuServe, the meter is running. Basic connect charges are figured by the minute

The membership support fee

The Executive Option

Connect time rates

and vary with your communications rate. Here are connect charges as of this writing:

Up to 300 bps	$6.00 per hour
1200/2400 bps	$12.50 per hour
9600 bps	$22.50 per hour

As you can see, 2400 bps is the most cost-effective rate (it is eight times faster than 300 bps at only twice the cost and is the same price as 1200 bps); however, if you make frequent file transfers, use the highest speed you can (9600 bps if possible). Get CompuServe telephone numbers for more than one bps rate, because different speeds are optimal for different applications.

Some areas of the system that are especially useful for learning are *free* of connect time charges. We will use these areas where possible, offering tips for making the most of your time spent online.

Communi-
cations
surcharges

- Communications surcharges, which pay for your network connection, vary from 30¢ per hour for CompuServe to $12 per hour for other public networks. Thus, it is generally best to use the CompuServe network; the telephone number that you are given by phone will usually connect you to it. Step 2 shows you how to find all available telephone numbers using CompuServe.

Additional
charges

- Certain CompuServe features entail surcharges. System menus will alert you to such charges in advance.

Signing On to CompuServe

Be sure your communications program is up and running at this point. Before you dial, turn on your program's log file to keep a record of this first session. (If you are using TELIX, you do this by pressing Alt-L and entering a log file name.) Compose a dialing-directory entry to store your standard settings for CompuServe. Figure 1.1 shows such an entry being made for TELIX. You reach this screen from the TELIX terminal-mode screen by pressing Alt-D, highlighting an entry, pressing **E** for edit, and filling in the

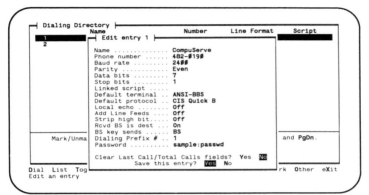

```
┤ Dialing Directory ├
        Name                      Number    Line Format    Script
  1                  ┤ Edit entry 1 ├
  2
              Name .............. CompuServe
              Phone number ...... 482-8198
              Baud rate ......... 2488
              Parity ............ Even
              Data bits ......... 7
              Stop bits ......... 1
              Linked script .....
              Default terminal .. ANSI-BBS
              Default protocol .. CIS Quick B
              Local echo ........ Off
              Add Line Feeds .... Off
              Strip high bit..... Off
              Rcvd BS is dest ... On
              BS key sends ...... BS
  Mark/Unma  Dialing Prefix # .. 1                    and PgDn.
              Password .......... sample:passwd

              Clear Last Call/Total Calls fields?  Yes  No
                        Save this entry?  Yes  No
Dial  List  Tog                                      rk  Other  eXit
Edit an entry
```

Figure 1.1: Making a dialing-directory entry

fields successively. Note the *data bits* and *parity* settings (7 bits, even parity), the *terminal emulation* (ANSI-BBS), and the default *file-transfer protocol* (CIS Quick B). Step 17 of this book will show you how to customize your account to take advantage of this terminal emulation.

It's time to dial the entry. (From the TELIX dialing directory, highlight the entry and press **D** for dial.) When you are connected, press Enter; when you see the network "Host Name:" prompt, enter the name **cis**, which stands for "Compuserve Information Service." (That is, type **cis** and press Enter. You can use either upper- or lowercase.) If you are logging on through a network other than CompuServe, follow the instructions that you received by phone. At the user ID and password prompts, enter the values in your subscription booklet. You will then be asked to provide your agreement number from the subscription booklet, your name and address, and other information, as well as to choose a billing method.

If you see a lot of nonsense characters popping up on your screen, you have a noisy telephone connection. You will have better luck if you sign off and dial the number again.

You will be given a permanent user ID and a temporary password. (Your permanent password will arrive in the mail). Be sure to note down your ID and password or preserve them in your log file. Be sure to keep your password private.

*An initial
menu*

You will then see a legend that brings you to the threshold of the service:

```
Please select
1 Online Tour (FREE)
2 Practice Forum (FREE)
3 CompuServe Information Service
Key choice: _
```

This screen illustrates the basic format of a CompuServe menu: a series of numbered options, followed by a prompt (here, "Key choice:"). A cursor will appear to the right of the prompt, where you can enter one of the option numbers. Other commands are usually available at the prompt.

*The main
menu*

If you feel adventuresome, try entering **1** or **2** now. (They will always be available to you through the main menu; you will have a chance to try out the Practice Forum in Step 4. These choices are free of connect charges.) Enter **3** for the main CompuServe menu, which will look like Figure 1.2. You may first see a news screen, which you can bypass by pressing Enter. This is Grand

```
CompuServe                    TOP

  1 Member Assistance (FREE)
  2 Find a Topic (FREE)
  3 Communications/Bulletin Bds.
  4 News/Weather/Sports
  5 Travel
  6 The Electronic MALL/Shopping
  7 Money Matters/Markets
  8 Entertainment/Games
  9 Hobbies/Lifestyles/Education
 10 Reference
 11 Computers/Technology
 12 Business/Other Interests

Enter choice number !_



  Alt-Z for Help | ANSI-BBS | 2400-E71 FDX |       |        | Online 00:01
```

Figure 1.2: The CompuServe main menu

Central Station for the CompuServe system, and you will be catching your first outbound train in the next step. Typical system prompts end with an exclamation point, as does the main menu prompt.

Signing Off from CompuServe

You can exit the system from any system prompt. Try this now by entering

bye

or *off*. When you see the "Host Name:" prompt again, enter **bye** a second time; your local node will hang up the line. You can then exit your communications program. (If you are using TELIX, press Alt-X.) Exiting the program will close and save your log file.

Always sign off CompuServe by entering **bye** or **off** at a system prompt. If you get hopelessly stuck, you can hang up the line (with TELIX, press Alt-H), but your connect time will continue for up to fifteen more minutes. You cannot stop this meter by signing on and off a second time.

With a bit of practice, you will soon be finding your way around CompuServe. The service is a hierarchy of menus, each leading to one or more lower-level menus, information screens, or actions. Think of a family tree, your DOS directory structure, or the pull-down menus in an application, and you will get the idea. In this step, we will examine this structure, as well as some shortcuts for getting around.

Since CompuServe periodically changes the order of menu choices, you might have to adapt to the screens you encounter. The wording of a menu item is more important than its number.

To begin, log on to CompuServe as you did in Step 1. This time, you will bypass the sign-up information and go to the main menu (or perhaps to a news menu).

Elements of a Menu

The top line of a menu always shows the name of the service (here, CompuServe) followed by the menu's name (sometimes called a *quick reference word* or *page number*). The numbered items that follow may be submenus or actions. A prompt near the bottom of the screen solicits your input, which will usually be a command and a carriage return (the Enter key on your keyboard, called <CR> by CompuServe). A prompt ending in an exclamation point is a CompuServe system prompt; you will encounter some special-purpose prompts later in this book.

Note the terms in parentheses (called *menu flags*) that follow some options, such as the term *FREE* following Member Assistance. Menu flags include:

   ($)   Designates added charges for a service. The
          charges should be explained under a help item.

   (E)   Designates a service available only if you have the
          Executive Service option.

(M)   Designates an item of merchandise that you have purchased.

Choosing Menu Items

When you choose a menu item, you get an overview of what is available under that item. You choose an item by entering its number.

Enter 1 to choose Member Assistance. (All topics under this submenu are free of connect charges; however, communications surcharges still apply). Follow this sequence to learn more about CompuServe rates:

1. Enter 7 for billing information. Note the information offered at the new menu, including information on the Executive Service option.

2. From this menu, enter 1 for current rates. Items in the new menu describe charges that may apply to your account. Note that the Executive Option is repeated from the previous menu—some items may appear in more than one menu.

3. From the new menu, enter 1 for connect-time rates.

4. From the following menu, enter 1 for the United States.

5. This choice shows an information screen listing hourly connect-time charges for various communications rates.

Now, try backing up the menu tree:

1. Press Enter from the "Last Page!" prompt to return to the preceding menu. (If there are several pages of information, leaf through them by pressing Enter.)

2. Press **M** to back up one menu; continue pressing **M** until you have returned to the menu titled *HELP*.

Try this sequence of commands to find your local telephone access number:

1. Enter **8** for telephone access numbers.

2. Enter **1** from the next menu to continue with this choice.

3. Enter a number in the next menu to specify your location (for example, choose *9* for the United States and Canada).

4. Enter **2** to search by city and state.

5. Enter your city and state at the prompt (for instance, *oakland, ca*).

6. You will be asked for a baud rate; enter **2400**.

7. CompuServe will display at least one entry like this:

City	State	Net	AC	Access #
Oakland	CA	CSM	415	482-0190

This entry offers a 2400-bps number on CompuServe as a local call from Oakland.

Most menu items include a word in capital letters. You can use the first three letters of this word in place of the item number. In Step 17, you will learn how you can speed through your CompuServe sessions by replacing menus with command prompts and entering commands such as these.

Moving in Broader Strides

You can jump to menu screens far removed from your current screen in one of two ways: by using the *T* command or the *go* command.

Going Right to the Top

The *T* command takes you directly to the top menu of a service. From a system menu, it returns you directly to CompuServe's TOP menu.

The T command

Enter **T** now to return to the TOP menu.

Going Places

The go
command

When you enter the *go* command followed by a keyword, you go directly to the screen associated with that keyword.

Enter **go rates** to go directly to the menu covering rate information, titled *BIL-4*.

The screen name itself always works as a keyword; for instance, you could have entered *go bil-4* in the example above. To cover additional familiar ground, enter **go connect** to see connect charges, and then enter **go phones** to revisit the menu of network numbers. Enter **go top** to return to the TOP menu. These commands work anywhere in the system.

You will learn to use the *find* command in the next step to show the keywords for any given topic.

Using Help Screens and Other Listings

You can view help screens—usually consisting of a command summary—from any "!" prompt. Before you do this, enter the command

```
set paged yes
```

to pause scrolling between each screenful of text. To view the help summary from the TOP menu, enter **H**. You can view successive screens by pressing Enter, or return to the previous menu by entering **M**. These screens describe further commands, not all of which are covered here.

Try the scrolling option, which is useful for capturing text to a log file. Enter the command

```
set paged no
```

and enter **H** again. To freeze the screen, press Ctrl-S; to allow scrolling to resume, press Ctrl-Q. To interrupt the display, press Ctrl-C; you will be prompted to press Enter to resume scrolling or to enter **M** to return to the previous menu. On other occasions, pressing Ctrl-C while scrolling will lead to a menu of options.

The **S** command will scroll text given by an option number or series of numbers. The syntax for this command is to enter **S**, followed by a space and an item number, two or more item numbers separated by commas, or a range of item numbers connected by a hyphen. Examples would be:

```
S 2
S 1,2
S 1-3
```

Log off your account now by entering **bye**.

Step 3

Finding a Topic

This step will introduce the ways that you can find a given topic or file on CompuServe. It will also serve as a quick introduction to some upcoming topics: forums, forum libraries, and downloads.

To begin, log on to your CompuServe account as you did in the previous step.

Finding a Topic

The Find a Topic menu is directly below the main menu, TOP. To search for a topic, enter **2** in TOP. The new menu will appear in this form:

```
1 Search for Topics of Interest
2 List ALL Indexed Topics
3 Explanation of Index
Enter choice ! _
```

You can see a complete list of CompuServe areas and their corresponding keywords (used together with the **go** command) by selecting the second menu choice. To page through this display by the screenful, enter **2** and press Enter after each screen. Alternatively, turn on your file log and capture a complete list of topics by entering the command **s 2**. Browsing through this list will show you the range of forums and other services available on CompuServe, ranging from computer and health forums to education and recreation services.

Keywords listed

Finding a Topic through a Menu

Try looking for a subject by entering **1** to choose the "Search for Topics of Interest" prompt. Then enter your topic at the "Enter topic <e.g. stock>:" prompt. For instance, if you enter **investment**, you will see several screens of CompuServe services relevant to investments. You can then identify a service of special interest and bring it up by entering **go**, followed by its keyword. Here are a few tips on searches:

- Enter the first few letters of a name (such as *invest*) to match all keywords beginning with those letters.

- Enter multiple words to look for areas that contain references to all the words.

- You can give a system command directly from a ":" prompt by prefacing it with a slash (/); for instance, **/t** returns you to the main menu.

Finding a Topic by Command

The *find* command is equivalent to the menu choice that you just tried but is available from any CompuServe system prompt. For instance, try entering

```
find pc software
```

to identify software services. You will see a multipage listing of such services. Note that forums named on the pattern "IBM *area* Forum" serve users of IBM-standard personal computers (ATs, 386s, PS/2s, and so on), and that forums named "PCVEN*x*" are manufacturers' shared forums.

Finding a Forum by Subject

Enter **go forums** for a menu of forum subjects. Pick a subject area by entering the item number. For instance, enter **1** to explore Aviation forums. If you enter **1** at the next menu that appears, you will be taken to the Aviation Forum itself.

Finding a File

CompuServe boasts a wealth of files for your PC—public domain and shareware programs, support files from computer manufacturers, information text files, and more. You can locate any of these files by using the IBM File Finder.

Bring up the IBM File Finder by entering **go ibmff** at a system prompt. (There is also a Macintosh File Finder, which you reach by entering **go macff**.) The main menu offers these choices, typical of such services:

```
1 About File Finder
2 Instructions for Searching
3 How to Locate Keywords
4 Access File Finder
5 Your Comments About File Finder
Enter choice ! _
```

Before you seek access to the service proper, you may want to browse items 1 and 2 to learn more about the options available to you. Then, enter **4** to open the File Finder, as shown in Figure 3.1. One way to search for a file is by product name, which will be one of the keywords associated with a file.

For this exercise, enter **1** to search by keyword and then enter **pkzip** to search for the popular file-archive utility. If you don't already have this shareware package, you will find it an invaluable tool in decompressing files you download from CompuServe.

Enter **1** again to view the files found. The first screen will look like Figure 3.2. Any program or file connected with PKZIP may also be

```
File Finder IBM

******************************************
Files are current as of: 08-Jul-91
******************************************
SEARCH BY:
 1 Keyword
 2 Submission Date
 3 Forum Name
 4 File Type
 5 File Extension
 6 File Name
 7 File Submitter (By User ID)
 8 Files Featured in FAVORITE FILES MANIA

Enter choice !_



 Alt-Z for Help | ANSI-BBS | 2400-E71 FDX |        |        | Online 00:00
```

Figure 3.1: File search options

listed. The utility package itself will be named PKZ*nnn*.EXE, where *nnn* is a version number. Entry 7 on the screen tells us that a current version of the program, PKZ110.EXE as of this writing, can be found in the IBM Communications forum (IBMCOM), in its Communications Utilities library. You can bring up this forum for a quick preview of forums and forum libraries, which we will examine in later steps.

Downloading a File from a Forum

To *download* a file is to copy it from a bulletin board service to your own PC. The following steps will download a file from a forum, provided you know its name and location in advance.

1.   Bring up the forum by entering **go ibmcom**. Page through any opening screens until you reach the main menu, which will look much like this:

IBM Communications Forum Forum Menu

1 INSTRUCTIONS

2 MESSAGES

3 LIBRARIES (Files)

4 CONFERENCING (0 participating)

5 ANNOUNCEMENTS from sysop

```
File Finder IBM

 1 BPROGA/Turbo Pascal v 5.x   CRCASM.ZIP
 2 BPROGA/Turbo Pascal v 5.x   ZIP-KI.ZIP
 3 BPROGA/Turbo Pascal v 5.x   ZIPPER.ZIP
 4 IBMAPP/Vertical Apps   RANG20.ZIP
 5 IBMAPP/Word Processing [A]   JOURNA.ZIP
 6 IBMBBS/BBS Doors [B]   AVIEW5.ZIP
 7 IBMCOM/Comm Utilities [C]   PKZ110.EXE
 8 IBMNEW/Library Tools [N]   PKZ110.EXE
 9 IBMNEW/Library Tools [N]   PRNDOC.ZIP
10 IBMNEW/Music [N]   WILL.ZIP
11 IBMOS2/General   PMZIP.ZIP
12 IBMOS2/General   ZIPQ05.ZIP
13 IBMPRO/DataCompression [P]   COMP8.COM
14 IBMPRO/DataCompression [P]   PKZ110.EXE
15 IBMPRO/DataCompression [P]   PKZOS2.EXE
16 IBMPRO/DataCompression [P]   UNZIP4.EXE
17 IBMPRO/Other Languages [P]   A2Z-S.EXE
18 IBMSYS/DOS Shells/Mgrs [S]   COMMAN.ZIP
19 IBMSYS/DOS Shells/Mgrs [S]   SAS24.ZIP
20 IBMSYS/DOS Shells/Mgrs [S]   SD-200.ZIP

Enter choice or <CR> for more !
Alt-Z for Help | ANSI-BBS | 2400-E71 FDX |          | Online 00:01
```

Figure 3.2: Some files keyed to PKZIP

```
6 MEMBER directory
7 OPTIONS for this forum
8 JOIN this forum
Enter choice ! _
```

2. If the Join option appears, join the forum by entering **8** and then entering your name. Joining a forum entails no obligations.

3. Enter **3** for the Libraries menu.

4. Enter **2** for the library section name that you learned in the File Finder, Comm Utilities.

5. Before you download a file, make sure it will fit on your drive. Enter **2** to view a Directory of files and browse for your file. Its size appears in the second column, after its name. Enter **M** after you have read the entry.

6. Enter **4** to Download the file. For this example, enter **5** next to choose the CompuServe Quick B protocol. Your communications program and CompuServe must be set to the same protocol.

7. Specify a name for the file. CompuServe will send this name along with the file. Files are easier to manage if you assign them their original CompuServe names.

Many communications programs can be set to download automatically when CompuServe initiates a CompuServe B or Quick B transfer. Using TELIX, for instance, you can set this option as follows: Press Alt-O from the terminal-mode screen, press **T** for Terminal options, press **M** for the CompuServe Quick B transfers option, highlight *Yes,* and press Enter.

If possible, avoid the XMODEM protocol for file transfers to or from CompuServe, as it is very slow when run over a network. If you must use XMODEM, look for a way to set "relaxed" XMODEM timing, which makes it more tolerant of delays.

8. If you are not set for automatic transfers, instruct your communications program to begin the download. For

instance, using TELIX, press Alt-R to receive a file (and note the space available), highlight the CIS Quick B protocol, and press Enter. If you have included this protocol in your CompuServe dialing-directory entry, you will find it already highlighted.

9. Watch the progress of the download on your program's file-transfer window. Press Enter when the download is finished.

Downloading TELIX

If you haven't yet obtained TELIX and want to use it for the rest of this book, you can find a copy just around the corner in the IBM Communications Forum. This example will show you a slightly different method for finding a file in a library.

1. Enter **5** to return to the Libraries list; enter **3** for Comm[unications] Programs.

2. Enter **1** at the following menu to Browse files in this section. Enter the keyword **telix**; press Enter to choose files of any date.

3. Browse the listings and look for files in the form T*nnn*-*n*.ZIP (for instance, T315-1.ZIP); these archive files will contain the TELIX package. (The first three digits indicate the version number, while the last is an archive-file sequence number.) As you encounter each file, enter **down** for a download and follow the transfer procedures that you have learned. (CompuServe will assume that you want to make CIS Quick B downloads for the rest of the session.)

4. When you have received all the archives (there will probably be three), enter **bye** to log off CompuServe.

Preparing Archived Software for Use

Archived shareware packages often contain numerous files. Keep these files together while you study the documentation and gain familiarity with the package.

Preparing PKZIP/PKUNZIP

You prepare PKZIP for use like this:

1. From DOS, create a directory to hold the archived files. Call it *PKZIP*. Change to that directory.

2. Run the self-unpacking archive by invoking its pathname from the command line, for instance

   ```
   c:\newfiles\pkz110
   ```

   if you downloaded PKZ110.EXE into a directory on your C drive called *NEWFILES*.

3. Set your printer to 66 lines-per-page and give the DOS command

   ```
   print *.doc
   ```

   to print a copy of the documentation. Study this documentation, including the licensing information. PKZIP creates and adds files to archives, while PKUNZIP extracts files from archives.

4. Include the directory PKZIP on your DOS path in your AUTOEXEC.BAT file, or else copy files with the EXE extension into a directory on your DOS path. If you don't know how to do this, consult your DOS documentation.

File archives come in a variety of formats. Try to obtain other archive software, such as ARC and LHA, for other archived programs that you download. Archive formats can be distinguished by file extension; for instance, ZIP for PKZIP/PKUNZIP, ARC for ARC, and LZH for LHA. Analogously, there are various archiving packages for the Macintosh.

Using TELIX

If you don't already have a full-featured communications program such as TELIX, you will find it invaluable for exploring upcoming features of CompuServe.

Put your new copy of PKUNZIP to use to unpack your new copy of TELIX. Follow these steps:

1. Prepare and log on to the TELIX directory as you did for PKZIP.

2. Unpack your downloaded archives into this directory by typing

   `pkunzip c:\newfiles\t315-*.`

   This command will place all the TELIX files in your new directory.

3. Print and study the documentation files (those with a DOC extension) as you did for the PKZIP documentation.

4. Prepare TELIX for use as described in its manual.

Forums are the hubs for social and information exchange on CompuServe. A *forum* is a community of users with a shared interest—be it computer graphics, health, aviation, or gardening. CompuServe forums are often major sources of technical support for microcomputer products. In this step, we will use the free Practice Forum to learn standard forum instructions and options.

To make learning easy, all forums are organized the same way. Each is a small computer bulletin board, with libraries of files, message sections, conference areas for live interaction, and *sysops,* or system operators, who manage the forum. Once you understand the basics, you can explore other CompuServe forums that interest you.

Forum organization

To begin, log on to your CompuServe account as usual.

Introducing Forums

You reach the Practice Forum by entering **1** for member assistance and then **6**. Page through the opening messages by pressing Enter. You'll see messages typical of forums. When you have read them all, you will reach the main menu. To join the forum, enter **8** and then enter your name as you did previously.

Reaching the Practice Forum

Understanding Forum Instructions

The numbered menu options shown at each forum level are shorthand for the available forum commands; there are other commands as well. For instance, try entering **ustatus** at the system prompt to learn who is currently logged on to the forum. You'll see users' IDs, names, and the forum sections they are using. If you recognize a user's ID, you can send him or her a message with the **send** command, described in Step 7. You can find out more about features like these in the Instructions menu.

You can tell where a user is calling from by reading the three-letter node abbreviation under "Nod." To understand these abbreviations, enter **go nodes** and then **3** to see a list of abbreviations, cities, and states.

Forum documents

Enter **1** from the main menu for the Instructions menu, shown in Figure 4.1. Here, choosing menu items 1 through 8 will lead to synopses of forum functions. Item 9 is a summary of all forum functions, while item 10 is a quick reference card and item 12 is a complete forum handbook.

It is more convenient to download items 9, 10, and 12 than to browse them.

To obtain a copy of the summary, turn on your communications program's file log (in TELIX, Alt-L), enter a filename, and enter **9**. The file will scroll past. You can download the Forum Reference Card and User's Guide the same way. Turn off and restart the file log, though, before you select a new item. When you are finished, press **T** to return to the main forum menu.

All downloads will be captured as ASCII text files, which you can print by entering **print** at the DOS prompt, followed by the name of the log file.

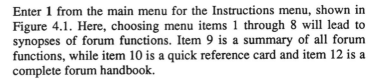

```
The Practice Forum(FREE) Instructions Menu

Instructions are available for:
  1 Overview
  2 Messages
  3 Libraries
  4 Conferencing
  5 Announcements
  6 Member directory
  7 Options
  8 Miscellaneous

  9 Complete HELP facility
 1Ø Forum Reference Card
 11 Forum User's Guide

Enter choice !_




 Alt-Z for Help │ ANSI-BBS │  24ØØ-E71 FDX │           │           │ Online ØØ:Ø1
```

Figure 4.1: The Instructions menu

Understanding Forum Announcements

The Announcements section contains items deemed interesting by the forum's sysops.

Bring up the announcements by entering **5** from the main forum menu. Try viewing each item by entering its number. Enter **T** to return to the main forum menu.

Understanding the Member Directory

The Member Directory option lets you create a directory entry, introducing you to other CompuServe members. It also allows you to search for information on other members.

Bring up the Member Directory by entering **6**. Enter **1** to add to your own entry. If you wish to, you can describe one or more of your interests. Each must be on its own line. When you are done, press Enter on a line by itself.

Try searching for users by interest. Enter **6** and then a keyword, such as *ecology*. You will see a list of users who have stated this interest. Like the "name" entry, you must exactly match the term provided by other users. Enter **T** to return to the forum main menu.

Understanding Forum Options

The Forum Options menu, shown in Figure 4.2, allows you to customize certain features of a forum. For instance, you can set the Initial option to bring up a particular menu when you first enter a forum. Or, you can instruct CompuServe to pause after viewing messages, or to pause only after messages addressed to you.

Try making a simple change. Enter **5** to add a character to your forum prompt. Then enter **^g** (caret + *G*) to add a bell to your forum prompts. Finally, enter **T** to return to the forum main menu; enter **S** to have the change apply to this session only. The prompt at the main menu should beep at you.

```
The Practice Forum(FREE) Options Menu

FORUM OPTIONS
 1 INITIAL menu/prompt [Forum]
 2 Forum MODE [MENU*]

MESSAGES OPTIONS
 3 PAUSE after messages [Always]
 4 NAME [Bob Campbell]
 5 Prompt CHARACTER []
 6 EDITOR [LINEDIT*]
 7 SECTIONS [...]
 8 HIGH msg read [103205]
 9 REPLIES info [Count]
10 TYPE waiting msgs [NO]
11 SKIP msgs you posted [NO]

LIBRARY OPTIONS
12 Library DISPLAY [Long]

Enter choice !_
```
```
 Alt-Z for Help | ANSI-BBS | 2400-E71 FDX |        |   | Online 00:01
```

Figure 4.2: Forum Options

This completes your introduction to CompuServe forums. Enter **bye** to log off CompuServe.

Step 5

Forum Message Sections

Using *forum messages,* you can correspond with other forum members or with a forum's sysops. Forum messages are invaluable for soliciting technical support on a product forum. In this step, you will learn how to find and respond to forum messages.

Forum messages are intended for public interchange. Even if a particular forum allows private messages, the contents can be viewed by the forum's sysops. Therefore, don't put confidential information in a message; send it via CompuServe's electronic mail system, described in Steps 8, 9, and 10.

To begin, sign on to the Practice Forum as you did in Step 4. Since the messages in a forum change continuously, this step will include generalized sample text.

Finding Messages

The message section offers two paths for finding messages. Enter **2** now from the forum main menu. The message menu looks like this:

```
Message age selection = [ALL]
1 SELECT (Read by section and subject)
2 READ or search messages
3 CHANGE age selection
4 COMPOSE a message
5 UPLOAD a message
Enter choice ! _
```

The first two selections allow you to view messages either by subject or by some specific criteria, such as messages addressed to you. Option 3 of this menu determines which messages will be available under options 1 and 2.

Enter **3** to see the selection criteria available, as shown here:

```
1 [*] NEW messages
2 [ ] ALL messages
3 [ ] STARTING message number
4 [ ] Number of DAYS
Enter choice ! _
```

The initial setting specifies messages posted since you last visited this section. You can change the setting to see all messages still on the system, messages numbered higher than *n*, or messages posted in the last *n* days. Try entering **2** to see the effect on subsequent menus. Then enter **M** to return to the main message menu.

Enter **2** to see the read menu, which takes this form:

```
Read
1 [ALL] messages
2 Message NUMBER
3 WAITING messages for you (0)
Search [new] messages
4 FROM (Sender)
5 SUBJECT
6 TO (Recipient)
Enter choice ! _
```

This example indicates that the caller has no messages. As a new forum member, you probably will not find this menu very interesting, because there won't be any messages for you. You might prefer to learn which subjects are hot and what discussions are taking place. To change your orientation in the message base, enter **M** to return to the message menu and then enter **1**. Here is a partial list of section names from the Practice Forum:

```
Section names (#subjs/#msgs)
1 General Information  (47/174)
2 Composing Messages  (19/41)
3 Reading Messages  (10/25)
4 Using the Libraries  (6/16)
```

```
5 How to Conference   (2/3)
11 My "TEST" Message   (41/74)
12 European Members   (8/71)
Enter choice(s) or ALL !  _
```

Of the numbers in parentheses, the first is the number of active
subjects under that section (governed by the age setting), and the
second is the total number of messages in that section. Each subject
is a message *thread;* that is, it is an original message to which there
are branching replies.

Enter a number to see some actual subjects, for example, 11 for "My
'TEST' Message." You will see

```
Section 11 - My "TEST" Message
1 Test Message   (1)
2 Testing   (3)
3 Practice Post   (1)
4 Another new user   (1)
```

Here, the number in parentheses is the number of messages in the
subject thread. Enter a number to view an actual message. You will
see the message's heading and body, followed by a prompt:

```
#107645 S11/My "TEST" Message
07-Oct-91 14:46:50
Sb: test
Fm: John Doe [SYSOP] 70000,0000
To: Jim Roe 70006,113
Jim,
   Your test message posted just fine. If you
need any assistance, please let me know.
->John
Press <CR> for next or type CHOICES !  _
```

The heading begins with a message and section number and subject,
followed by the date and time the message was posted. The time is
your local time. If there are more messages in the thread, you can
see them by pressing Enter.

Sending Messages

At this point, you are almost ready to send a message of your own. Enter **choices** to see your basic options:

```
1 REPLY with same subject
2 COMPOSE with new subject
3 REREAD this message
4 NEXT reply
5 NEXT SUBJECT
8 Subject menu
9 Section menu
Enter choice ! _
```

The first two selections take you directly to CompuServe's online editor, where you could formulate a reply. The difference between the two is that if you *compose* a message, the system will prompt you for a recipient and a subject, whereas, if you *reply,* they will be taken from the previous message.

Enter a reply now, even if you don't want to send it.

Entering a message

At the "Enter message" prompt, you can type a reply. This is a primitive text editor—press Enter when you reach the right edge of your screen. If you see a mistake on your current line, backspace over and correct it. If you see one on a preceding line, leave it to edit later. Enter /exit on a line by itself when you are finished. You will then be given the choices

```
1 POST message on board
2 EDIT message
3 TYPE message
5 CANCEL message compose
Enter choice ! _
```

Editing a message

Enter **2** to see the editing options. You can specify certain characters in a line for substitution. You can also replace, delete, or insert whole lines by line number. Choose the Type option if you are not sure which line you want to edit. When you are ready, press Enter to return to the previous menu. At this point, if you really want to send your reply, enter **1**. Otherwise, enter **5** to delete the message and **Y** to confirm. Enter **M** twice to return to the message menu.

Uploading Your Messages

You can write better messages *and* save time and expense by composing them prior to logging on and then uploading them. To *upload* is to copy a file from your computer to CompuServe. Compose the message on your word processor and save it as an ASCII text file. Then log on and choose the upload option by entering **5** at the main message menu. You will be asked to choose a protocol and give the source filename. You will then be prompted for a recipient and subject and given a chance to post your message. Forum messages are limited to 2500 characters and 96 lines.

When you are finished, log off the system as usual.

Save money by uploading messages!

Forum libraries comprise much of the information stored on Compu-Serve, some of which you can find and read online. Most library files, though, are in formats that are unwieldy or impossible to peruse online, and must be downloaded. In this step, you will learn how to browse library files and download those of interest.

To begin, log onto CompuServe and the Practice Forum as you have done in the previous two steps.

Browsing Library Files

You can reach the libraries menu by entering **3** from the forum's main menu. As of this writing, the Practice Forum had three subject areas:

```
1 Forum Help & Info
2 Forum Scripts/Pgms
3 New Library Info
Enter choice ! _
```

Bring up "Forum Help & Info" files by entering **1**. This leads to the standard library section menu:

```
Forum Help & Info
1 BROWSE Files
2 DIRECTORY of Files
3 UPLOAD a File (FREE)
4 DOWNLOAD a File to your Computer
5 LIBRARIES
Enter choice ! _
```

You saw in Step 3 how to download a file directly from this menu. The menu offers other means for finding and obtaining files.

Enter **1** to browse the files in this section. Press Enter to see files in the current library. Press Enter at the "Enter keywords" and "Oldest files in days" prompts so that you can see all files in sequence. You will encounter a file listing like the one in Figure 6.1.

The top line of this listing is the User ID of the original contributor. The next line contains the file's name, type, size in bytes, number of times that it has been read or downloaded, and date of uploading.

The file's extension is an important clue to its contents. Files with extensions such as LST (list), TXT (text), DOC (document), or CAT (catalog) are text files that you can view online, capture to a log file, or download. Other files, such as archives with extensions like ZIP or ARC, or graphics files with extensions like GIF, are *binary* files that you must download with a file-transfer protocol such as CIS Quick B. Note the file's size and check that you have enough disk space for the download, which will consume time directly proportional to the file's size for a given protocol and baud rate.

Section
catalogs

Sometimes the two most recent files in a section will contain a current list of files. Their names may include an abbreviation of the forum name, a section number, and the extension CAT or ARC. You can view or download these files as described below.

Before downloading a file, always note its size and make sure you have room for it on your disk.

```
Press <CR> for next or type CHOICES !

[76702,542]      Lib: 1
FORUMS.LST/Asc  Bytes:  13347, Count:  466, 22-Jul-91

    Title   : Complete list of forums
    Keywords: FORUMS GO PAGE ID QUICK REF WORDS INDEX

    Complete list of CompuServe Forums as of July 21, 1991.

    Included for each forum:
    - Gateway Code
    - Quick Reference Words

    (see SECTNS.ARC for a larger version that includes Message Section
    and Library Names)

                    Prepared - Ed Girou, PRACTICE forum

Press <CR> for next or type CHOICES !
  Alt-Z for Help | ANSI-BBS |  2400-E71 FDX |            | Online 00:19
```

Figure 6.1: A file listing

The listing includes a title composed by the sysop, followed by a list of keywords and descriptions. You can use keywords to search for files in the IBM File Finder. In a moment, you will have a chance to see how keywords work in the library section menu.

If there is more than one screenful of description, you will see the prompt

```
Press <CR> for more ! _
```

When you have reached the end of the listing, the prompt will read

```
Press <CR> for next or type CHOICES ! _
```

If you want to take action on this file, the easiest command to remember is **choices**. Enter it now to see the following action menu:

```
The Practice Forum (FREE) Library Disposition
1 READ this file
2 DOWNLOAD this file
3 DESCRIPTION
4 RETURN to library menu
Enter choice or <CR> for next ! _
```

You can read the file by entering **1**. It will scroll by continuously. (Recall that you can use Ctrl-S and Ctrl-Q to suspend and resume scrolling.) When you have seen all of the file, you will receive the prompt

```
Press <CR>! _
```

The heading and the prompt for choices will then redisplay.

Downloading Library Files

Enter **choices** again to redisplay the menu. This time, enter **2** to download the file. Enter a number to specify a file-transfer protocol, such as **5** for CompuServe QB. Provide a file name for your computer. When prompted (for Quick B, you'll see a character like a club on a deck of cards), tell your communications program to begin the transfer. When the transfer is finished, press Enter.

If your communications program has difficulty with file transfers under these conditions (for instance, you get garbage onscreen or experience lockups), you may want to change your data bit and parity settings. Step 17 will show you how.

Press Enter until you find another file with a text extension. You may find one with heading information similar to Figure 6.2.

This time, make an ASCII transfer. ASCII transfers, although less reliable than protocol transfers, are handy for short text files. Also, they are sometimes the only means of transfer available.

Capturing
a text file

- Before you begin entering commands, start a log file (as described in Step 1) or prepare for an ASCII download. If using TELIX, press Alt-R, press **A** for ASCII, note your free disk space, and enter a name for the new file.

- Give a shortened form of the read command right from the "CHOICES" prompt. All you need to do is enter **R**.

When the transfer is finished, turn off the file log or terminate the ASCII transfer. (Esc will end an ASCII download from TELIX.)

```
(see SECTNS.ARC for a larger version that includes Message Section
and Library Names)

                     Prepared - Ed Girou, PRACTICE forum

Press <CR> for next or type CHOICES !

[76702,542]
COMPRS.DOC/Asc  Bytes:   8868, Count:  866, 13-Jun-91(13-Jun-91)

   Title   : Generic information about compressed files
   Keywords: ARC ZIP ZOO LZH SIT ARCHIVE COMPRESSION DECOMPRESSION HELP

   Text file explaining Compressed Files (i.e. ARC, ZIP, ZOO, LZH, SIT
   file extensions).  Generic information with pointers to the appropriate
   support forum, library, and file names for the decompression utilities.
   Covers Apple 128K IIe, IIc, IIgs, Amiga, Atari, Commodore 8-bit, DOS (IBM),
   and Macintosh platforms.

Press <CR> for next or type CHOICES !
 Alt-Z for Help | ANSI-BBS |  2400-E71 FDX |          |          | Online 00:05
```

Figure 6.2: Another file listing

Now, let's try another experiment:

If you have tried multiple file transfers during a session, you have noticed that CompuServe asks you to name a protocol for the first transfer and then uses your initial choice for all later transfers. But what do you do if your first choice doesn't work out? Fortunately, you can change protocols "on the fly" with special command abbreviations.

Changing protocols

For instance, to switch to a Ymodem protocol, enter this command at the prompt for choices:

```
down/proto:ymo
```

Here, *down* is shorthand for *download,* and *ymo* is shorthand for *Ymodem.*

You can abbreviate other protocols like this:

KER	for Kermit
XMO	for Xmodem
A	for ASCII
B	for CompuServe B
B+	for CompuServe B+
QB	for CompuServe Quick B

Use the form of CompuServe B that is supported by your communications program. When you have made the transfer and are prompted for choices, enter **M** to return to the library section menu.

Other Library Options

The rest of the step will give you a quick look at other options in a library section menu.

Browsing by Keyword

Enter **1** from the menu to browse; this time, enter **messages** at the keywords prompt to view listings that have *Messages* as a keyword. When prompted for "Oldest files in days," press Enter; some files here may be fairly old. (Enter **15**, for instance, to browse listings uploaded in the last fifteen days.) Press Enter to browse all matching files; you will soon be returned to the menu.

Look for a file listing including the keyword *Emoticons* and capture the text file; this will explain the cryptic visual devices that CompuServe users sometimes use to personalize their messages.

The File Directory

At the library section menu, enter **2** to see a directory of short file listings such as these:

[76702,542]

FORUMS.LST	22-Jul-91 13347	Accesses: 122
SECTNS.ARC/binary	22-Jul-91 74213	Accesses: 71
COMPRS.DOC	13-Jun-91	Accesses: 585
	(13-Jun-91) 8868	

The directory consists of message headings arranged by the User ID of the contributor. If you know a file's name, you can spot it here much more quickly than by browsing. You can return to the section menu by entering **M** at any time. Press **M** after viewing a page or two of listings.

Changing Libraries

Enter **5** to return to the libraries menu from this section. This command saves you a step when moving from one library section to another; without it, you would have to enter **M** for the main forum menu and then **3** for the libraries menu.

Pick another library section and browse its files as you did those of the first section. Then log off CompuServe as usual.

Forum Conferences

15

Conferences are live interactions over the CompuServe network. Using a forum conference, you can rendezvous with friends or have spontaneous conversations with other forum participants. This step will show you how to find and join conferences.

To try out the ideas in this step, you may want to find a confederate. If so, sign on to CompuServe from separate PCs, enter a prearranged forum, and move to a conference room, as described below. You both can use the same CompuServe ID.

Find a friend

Otherwise, find a forum conference in progress and join in. Many forums have regularly scheduled conferences.

Finding a Conference Room

Find an interesting forum by using the **find** command, sign on, and join it. Have your friend do the same. The example below uses the Datastorm forum, which offers support for Datastorm, Inc. products, including PROCOMM PLUS, a communications program.

Conferencing is choice 4 on the forum main menu. The menu item includes the number of users currently in conference. Enter **4** to begin. Conferences include varying numbers of public communications areas called *rooms*. The menu, illustrated below, shows how many users are in each room:

The conferencing section

```
The DATASTORM Forum CO Rooms Menu
Conference Rooms Available (# users):
2 Break Room   (0)
3 Tech's Lounge   (0)
4 Test Cube   (0)
Enter choice ! _
```

This is the basic conference model: a number of public rooms, in which users gather and converse. When conferencing, you can find out who is in a room, move from room to room, eavesdrop on other

The conference model

rooms, conduct private conferences, or effectively whisper into the ear of another conference user.

Finding out who is on a forum

Note that you are still at a command prompt. Enter **users** to find out who is signed onto this forum. You will see a list like this one:

User	User ID	Nod	Area	Name
1	00000,0000	MNN	Lib	John Doe
2	12345,777	OKD	Forum	Chris Burmester
3	99999,9999	AAK	Mes	Jane Roe
4	12345,678	OKD	Forum	Bob Campbell

The first column shows each users' *job number,* an arbitrary number assigned them when they sign on to the forum. In addition, you are informed of users' IDs, nodes of origin, sections (libraries, main forum menu, etc.), and names.

Sending a message in a forum

You can send a message to your friend using his or her job number. Type **send**, followed by the number and your message, all on one line. For instance, enter

```
send 2 Join me in Room 2 of the Conference area
```

to arrange a meeting. (If your friend is using the same ID, you may have to try both job numbers.) Your friend will see your message, prefaced by a tag with your name and job number. Now go into your chosen room by entering its number (**2** in the example).

Interacting in a Conference

Conference messages and commands

Note that there is no conference prompt; what you type will be sent to all other occupants of the room when you hit Enter. There is one exception: any text you preface with a forward slash will be read as command input to the conferencing software. For instance, enter **/name** to set the way your name will be displayed to conference participants. You will be prompted:

What's your name

Enter your first name.

Now, try sending a message. If you say, for instance:

Hello, out there!

your message will appear on the other participants' screens like this:

(2-4,Bob)Hello, out there!

Make a few brief exchanges like this. Note the tag on incoming messages. The first number is the sender's room number; the second, his or her job number. You can learn about other participants in the conference room much as you learned about forum participants at the forum main menu. For instance, enter **/users** to find out who is currently in conference on this forum. You will see a display like this:

User	User ID	Nod	Area	Name
2	12345,777	OKD	Rm 2	Chris
4	12345,678	OKD	Rm 2	Bob

This is equivalent to the forum list you saw earlier, only now the Area heading tells you the room number within the forum. You can learn your own job number by entering **/job**.

Sometimes a message will arrive while you are typing one of your own, making it difficult to see what you have typed. You can clear your input and start over by pressing Ctrl-U or place what you have already typed on a new line by pressing Ctrl-V. You can also press Ctrl-U before sending a slash (/) command to ensure that it is read as a command and not a message.

Sending a message in a conference

Monitoring Another Room

You can *monitor* conversations in one or two other rooms. Messages from these rooms will appear on your screen, but your own messages will appear only to users in or monitoring your current room. For instance, enter /**mon 3 4** to monitor the other two rooms in the example forum. Then enter /**unmon 4** to stop monitoring the Test Cube.

*Conference
activity*

You can get a general idea of conference activity by entering /**status**; the system will show you how many users are in each occupied room, for example:

(2) 2#

Your current room will then be flagged with a pound sign; rooms that you are monitoring will be flagged with an asterisk.

Sending a Private Message

To send a private message to another user on the conference, enter the conference command /**send *n message*,** where *n* is the recipient's job number. For instance, user 4 might enter:

/send 2 Do you hear what this guy is saying?

User 2 will then be the only user to see the message. It will be prefaced by the job number, name, and room number of its source.

Moving to a Private Room

Any time you are conferencing with several other people, you can invite one or more of them into a *private* conference, where you will not be joined or monitored by others. For this practice session, invite your friend to a private conference by entering **invite** and your friend's job number. The conference software will create a *group* or private room for you. It will instruct you on how to leave a group at the same time:

```
% Entering group - /BREAK exits group - /USERS
lists group members
% Inviting user 2 to join group
```

The percent sign denotes a message from the conference software. Your friend will see the message:

```
% User 4 [12345,678] Bob invites you to
/JOIN 4
```

To which your friend should respond /**join 4**. Your friend will then receive the same "% Entering group" prompt and you can converse as before. When you enter /**break**, you will return to the public room. Always send a goodbye message before leaving a room.

Now that you have tried conferencing, you may wish to try CompuServe's popular CB Simulator. You can reach it by entering **go cb**. The CB (Citizen's Band) simulator is subdivided into "bands" and "channels" instead of "rooms." Otherwise, most of the commands are the same as for a forum conference.

Getting help

You can bring up a list of conference commands at any time by entering /**help**. If you want to see a brief description of how a command works, simply type its name at the prompt.

Signing Off

To sign off a conference and return to the main forum menu, enter /**exit**. Alternatively, use one of the system-navigation commands. For instance, enter /**go mail** to jump directly from the forum conference to CompuServe's Electronic Mail service, which we will examine in the next step.

Enter /**bye** now to log off CompuServe.

Step 8

Sending Electronic Mail

30

CompuServe features a complete e-mail (electronic mail) service. This service provides you with a means of sending messages not only to CompuServe subscribers, but also to international e-mail networks. In this step, we will explore the basics of sending e-mail messages.

Using the Directory

To send mail, the first thing you need is an address. For fellow CompuServe subscribers, that address is their user ID. You have already seen commands (such as *users* and forum directory commands) that yield user IDs. You can also use the Member Directory to find a user ID if you know at least part of the subscriber's name.

Bring up the Member Directory (which is free of connect charges) by entering **go member** from a system prompt. The main menu takes this form:

```
CompuServe (FREE) DIRECTORY
MEMBER DIRECTORY
 1 Explanation
 2 Member Directory Search
   (U.S. and Canada)
 3 Member Directory Search
   (International)
 4 Include/Exclude This User ID
Last page, enter choice ! _
```

Like any user, you can opt to have your own name excluded from the directory. First enter **4** for "Include/Exclude this ID" from the main directory menu and then enter **2** to choose the menu item "Do NOT List in directory."

Begin your search by entering **2**. At the prompt,

```
Last name (<CR> to exit): _
```

enter a name, such as **Clark**. At the following prompt,

```
First name begins with (e.g. JOH): _
```

enter a first name or fragment thereof, such as **dav**. The search will include any first name beginning with these three letters, such as *Dave* or *David*. Enter enough of the name that you don't get too many possibilities.

In this example, too many subscribers (more than fifteen) have names that match our search string, so you are prompted to enter a state abbreviation. Type **ca**, and you will see a set of names, cities, states, and user IDs.

Once you have a user ID, you can send a message. For this practice session, try composing and sending a message to a friend or to yourself (mailing it to your own user ID). Bring up the e-mail service by entering **go mail** from any system prompt. The mail main menu takes this form:

```
CompuServe Mail Main Menu
   *** No mail waiting ***
2 COMPOSE a new message
3 UPLOAD a message
4 USE a file from PER area
5 ADDRESS Book
6 SET options
9 Send a CONGRESSgram ($)
Enter choice ! _
```

Using the Address Book

Before you actually send a message, take a few moments to try out the Address Book. This is a handy place to store names and addresses of your frequent correspondents. When you send a message to someone in your Address Book, you need supply only the recipient's name. CompuServe takes care of the address. Activate it by entering **5** from the main menu. It will look like this:

```
CompuServe Mail Address Book
 1 INSERT an entry
 2 CHANGE an entry
 3 DELETE an entry
 4 LIST Address Book
 5 Enter/Change your NAME/Postal Address
Enter choice ! _
```

To create a new entry from the main menu, enter **1**. Note that you are shown which entry number you are adding. At the "Name" prompt, enter your own name. At the prompt, "*Your Name*'s address," enter your user ID. The Address Book consists of pairs of names and IDs, allowing CompuServe to look up addresses for any recipients you name.

CompuServe addresses

Try adding another new entry, this time using the author's name. At the prompt, "Bob Campbell's address," enter

Other addresses

```
>INTERNET: rac@violet.berkeley.edu
```

This address is on another mail system. The information after the colon is a standard Internet address naming a user ("rac"), system ("violet"), and site ("berkeley"). Enter all characters literally, including the initial angle bracket and the space after the colon. Enter more names and addresses if you like, and then press Enter at a name prompt to return to the Address Book main menu.

Include postal addresses in your Address Book to send mail directly from CompuServe. For more information, see Step 9.

Enter **4** to list your entries. Press Enter after viewing them. You can change or delete an entry from the menu by number. If you choose an entry by number, you will be prompted to accept or to replace first the name and then the address. In both cases, just press Enter or you will enter a new name or address.

Listing Address Book entries

Add your own name and postal address to the Address Book by entering **5**. You will be prompted for:

- Your full name

- An optional title or company name

- Your address

- An optional second line for your address

- Your city

- Your state

- Your zip code

Enter **N** when you have reistered your address correctly, and then enter **M** to return to the mail main menu.

Composing and Sending a Message

First, enter **2** from the main menu. At the prompt,

```
Enter message. (/EXIT when done) _
```

Enter a few lines of text like this:

```
1: Hi Your name,
2: This is just a test message to try out
this editor.
3: Be seeing you.
4: /exit
```

You can include a greeting and a salutation, but leave out the inside and return addresses. As you type each line, press Enter when your text reaches the right margin. When you are done, type **/exit** on a line by itself and press Enter.

You will then see the mail send menu, which looks like this:

```
CompuServe Mail Send Menu
For current message
```

```
1 SEND
2 EDIT
3 TYPE
4 TYPE/POSTAL
5 FILE DRAFT copy
6 SEND with /RECEIPT ($)
Enter choice ! _
```

Enter **3** to type your message and see how it looks. If you spot a mistake, enter **2** and edit the message. To send the message, enter **1**. At the "Send to" prompt, enter your name as you recorded it in the Address Book, allowing the system to supply the address. Enter a subject as prompted. Once you confirm that the address is correct as displayed, the message will be sent. If the recipient is a CompuServe subscriber, he or she will receive the message in a few minutes.

When you have finished exploring e-mail, log off CompuServe as usual.

In this step, we will further explore CompuServe's e-mail system. Advanced features include Congressgrams, uploading files, transmitting files to other subscribers, and sending mail to other entities, such as networks, MCI Mail, FAX machines, or post offices.

Pre-Composing and Uploading Your Messages

When you have a lengthy message or one you want to edit carefully, it is best to compose it offline and then upload the message to CompuServe's e-mail. This practice will save you connect-time and place the editing features of your word processor at your fingertips. Remember, though, that you must save your message as an ASCII file.

You can also send e-mail messages to the personal file area, which will be covered in Step 16.

Sending Congressgrams

One unique and useful CompuServe service is Congressgrams. These are messages CompuServe will laserprint and deliver to the President, the Vice-President, or a member of Congress for $1.00. If you have been meaning to write your congressperson but haven't gotten around to it, this service makes it very easy.

Practice sending a message to one of your national senators:

1. Log on to CompuServe and bring up e-mail by entering **go mail**.

2. Enter **9** to send a Congressgram.

3. Enter **2** for the Senate.

4. Page through the list of states and enter your state's number (such as **5** for California).

5. Jot down information on your recipient (such as the proper spelling of his or her name) and press Enter.

6. Enter **M** to return to the Members of Congress menu and then enter **4** to compose your Congressgram.

7. Enter the recipient's name with proper capitalization, and answer the query

    `Is recipient the President, Vice President,`
    `a Senator or Representative? (P, VP, S or`
    `R) : _`

    by entering **S** for Senator.

8. If the beginning of the inner address is correct, for instance

    `To: The Honorable Alan Cranston (Senator)`

    enter **Y**.

9. The e-mail system will display a message and a line scale. This is as far as we can go without actually sending a message.

There are special limitations on the length and column width of Congressgrams. Most messages can be 50,000 characters long, with 80 characters-per-line; however, Congressgrams are limited to 69 characters-per-line and 88 lines-per-message. CompuServe mail will automatically enter the recipient's address, the salutation, and the closing.

10. Enter **/exit** to leave off message entry. You will be given a prompt:

    `% Message workspace empty`

    Press Enter and then enter **M** to return to the main mail menu.

Uploading an ASCII File

To experience ASCII uploads, send a message to yourself as you did in the preceding step. First log off CompuServe to compose the message.

Your communications program may allow you to run your text editor without exiting the program (this process is called *shelling out*). Some products even have "hot keys" to invoke other programs. Set up TELIX to shell out to your editor by following these steps:

1. Press Alt-O for the Setup menu.
2. Press **F** for "Filenames and Paths."
3. Press **H** for the Editor Name option and enter the name of your editor with its file extension (for instance, **ed.exe** for PC-Write). Include its drive and path if it is not included in your DOS PATH.

You can then start your editor by pressing Alt-A.

Once your editor is running, write a message to yourself and save it as an ASCII text file. Exit the editor as usual. Now follow these steps to carry out the ASCII transfer:

1. Log on to CompuServe, go to e-mail, and enter **2** to compose a message.
2. When prompted to enter your message, begin the ASCII upload. From TELIX, press Alt-S and **A**, and enter your file's path and name.
3. When the transfer is finished, enter **/exit**.
4. Enter **1** to send your message and enter your own name or user ID at the "Send to" prompt.

Making a Binary Upload

Any files that are not text-only are called *binary files*; these cannot be transmitted through ASCII transfers. Instead, you must do a *binary upload.*

Choose a file in advance for this exercise. Use your communications program's directory-listing command to locate a file (in TELIX, press Alt-F, then **F**, and enter a path). A good choice is a word-processed file in a special format. (This requires that you and your recipient have the same word processor.) Send this file as another message to yourself:

1. After returning to the mail main menu, enter **3** to upload a message.

2. Pick a file-transfer protocol—for instance, enter **6** to pick Quick B.

3. Enter **3** for a binary transfer.

4. Enter your file's name.

5. If you are not set for automatic CompuServe B transfers, start your local upload procedure when prompted.

6. When the transfer is finished, press Enter. For the recipient, enter your name as written in the address book.

The New Pony Express

In addition to uploading files, e-mail allows you to send mail to other services or to post mail directly from CompuServe. There are restrictions to these types of messages, though:

- Mail directed outside CompuServe must be limited to text files.

- Addresses for other services must begin with a right angle bracket, followed by the name of the service, a colon, a space, and then the address in the form required by that service. You made an entry like this for my address in the preceding step. To learn more about e-mail addressing, see *!%@::, A Directory of Electronic Mail Addressing & Networks* by Adams and Frey (O'Reilly and Associates, Inc, Sebastopol, California.). This book is updated frequently.

- You can read about address forms, special limitations, and additional charges by entering **help** at the mail main menu and then choosing a topic, such as **mcimail**. Enter **help postal description** for an overview of CompuServe's postal services.

Try these exercises to practice different forms of addresses:

1. Create an Address-Book entry for a friend: Enter your friend's name and then enter **>postal**. Enter your friend's mailing address as prompted. Compose a brief message online and send it as prompted. It will cost you $1.50 for a one-page domestic mailing.

2. Compose and send a message destined for another e-mail system, such as MCI or Internet. If you like, you can tell the author what you think of this book so far, using the address that appears in the preceding step.

Now sign off CompuServe and await your messages. You will learn how to retrieve them in Step 10.

Step 10

Receiving Electronic Mail

This step will give you some practice in reading and downloading mail from CompuServe and briefly describe how to set your mail options.

By now, you have sent at least two e-mail messages to yourself, one text and one binary, as described in Step 9. If you just sent them, wait a few minutes, then log on to your CompuServe account. Just before the main menu appears, you will be greeted by the message:

```
You have Electronic Mail waiting.
```

Bring up the mail main menu by entering **go mail** as before.

Reading Your Mail

When you have un-read or saved mail,

```
1 READ mail, n messages pending
```

appears on this menu. Enter **1** to see your messages. The read menu will show the sender's name and the subject, like so:

```
CompuServe Mail Read Menu
1 John Q. Reader/Sample Text Message
2 John Q. Reader/Test Document
* Binary *
0 READ ALL 2 messages
Last page.  Enter choice or M for CompuServe
Mail main menu ! _
```

Enter **0** to see each of your new messages in succession. If your first message is a text message, it will appear. A typical text message will have a header, showing when and by whom it was sent and the subject. If the message has more than one page, you will be prompted to press Enter. At the end, the following prompt appears:

```
Last page. Enter command or <CR> to continue ! _
```

For a menu of commands, press Enter.

All commands can be entered at the "Last page:" prompt. You can even use an abbreviated form, such as *del* for the Delete command.

The action menu takes this form:

```
CompuServe Mail Action Menu
** John Q. Reader/Sample Text Message **
1 DELETE this message
2 FILE in PER area
3 FORWARD
4 REREAD message
5 REPLY
6 SAVE in mailbox
7 DOWNLOAD message
Enter choice or <CR> to continue ! _
```

Message
options

With this menu, you can do the following:

1. Delete the message.

2. Transfer the message to your personal file area (described in Step 16).

3. Forward the message to another subscriber. This choice gives you the option of preceding it with a comment, which is treated as an original message (see Step 8).

4. Reread the message.

5. Reply to the message.

6. Save the message in your mailbox. It will then be there when you next sign on and bring up mail.

7. Download the message, which we will do shortly.

8. Bypass the menu by pressing Enter, which will store but not save the message. CompuServe will delete unsaved messages ninety days after they are sent.

Regardless of what action you take, you will ultimately be prompted to dispose of the message in some way.

Downloading a Message

To download the message, type **4** and initiate the transfer. (Using TELIX, press Alt-R to receive the file, press **A** for ASCII, and enter a filename.) Press Enter to send the reread command. When the "Last page:" prompt appears, end your download (in TELIX, by pressing Esc). Then press Enter to return to the action menu and dispose of the message (by deleting it, for example).

An ASCII download

CompuServe cannot display binary mail, so if your second message is a binary file, you will see a normal header followed by the note,

Binary downloads

%Message is Binary

in place of the message body. In order to read this message, you must download it using a regular file-transfer protocol. Press Enter at the "Last page:" prompt and enter **7** for Download at the action menu. You will be prompted for a file-transfer protocol, and you will be shown a prompt such as the following one:

```
2 John Q. Reader/Test Document
08-Aug-91 19:55 PDT 12345,678 Length 16837
* Binary *
1 messages and 16837 characters ready for
download
Enter a filename for your computer: _
```

This indicates the source of the file and its length. It also asks you to assign a filename. Supply a descriptive name (and a path, if needed) and hit Enter, and CompuServe will begin the transfer. When the transfer is finished, press Enter and you will return to the mail action menu. Delete the original message; if you have no further messages, you will return to the mail main menu.

Customizing E-Mail

You can customize e-mail by entering **6** from the main menu. The options menu is shown here:

```
CompuServe Mail Options Menu
[ ] Represents Current Setting
(yes/no options toggle)
1 EDITOR uses line numbers [YES]
2 MODE of operation is [MENU]
(MENU, PROMPT, COMMAND)
3 Output is PAGED [YES]
Enter choice ! _
```

The current values are shown in square brackets You change a Yes/No option (here, options 1 and 3) by entering its number. You change a multiple-choice option (here 2) by entering its number and choosing from a menu. This menu allows you to do the following:

1. Set the editor to suppress line numbers (it then displays only the text). This lets you see more columns onscreen.

2. Set the mode of operation to Menu, which yields menus, Prompt, which results in a long prompt of options, like this:

   ```
   SCAn, REAd, COMpose, ADDress or HELp! _
   ```

   or Command, which results in the terse prompt,

   ```
   Mail! _
   ```

   To use these prompts effectively, you must be familiar with the commands.

3. Set output to be paged. As you read your messages, you are prompted to press Enter after each screenful. If this option is set to No, messages will scroll past without interruption.

If you set option 3 to No, you can display and capture all text messages at once. In my book *Understanding PROCOMM PLUS* (SYBEX, 1991) there is a script file that will automatically sign on to CompuServe, collect all new messages, and sign off again.

To leave the settings menu, press Enter and then enter **Y** or **N** when asked whether you want the new value to be permanent.

This ends your introduction to e-mail on CompuServe. You can sign off as usual at this point.

Step 11

News Information

In this step, we will explore CompuServe's news services, which give you the world's major wire services on tap. These are the same wire bureaus (UPI, AP, Reuters, etc.) that feed news stories to the broadcast media, so you are assured of getting the latest news, sports, and business reports.

To access CompuServe's most comprehensive and flexible service, the Executive News Service, you must sign up for the Executive Service Option, which entails additional charges. The other services are free of surcharges.

To reach the master news menu, log on to your CompuServe account and enter **go news**. You can reach any of these services directly by using their keywords.

The master menu offers the following options:

The news master menu

```
News/Weather/Sports NEWS
  1 Executive News Service ($)
  2 NewsGrid
  3 Associated Press Online
  4 Weather
  5 Sports
  6 The Business Wire
  7 Newspaper Library
  8 Entertainment News/Info
  9 Online Today Daily Edition
Enter choice ! _
```

Using NewsGrid

NewsGrid offers quick access to world, U.S., and business news, as well as to stock market updates. To reach NewsGrid, enter **2** from the news main menu (or enter **go newsgrid** from any system prompt).

NewsGrid is free of surcharges!

The NewsGrid main menu takes this form:

```
NEWSGRID (sm)
  1 US/World Headline News
  2 US Business Headline News
  3 World Business Headline News
  4 Market Update
  5 Search by Keyword
  6 How to use NewsGrid
A product of Comtex Scientific Corp.
Enter choice ! _
```

Scanning News Stories

The first three NewsGrid menu options allow you to scan stories by topic and read those of interest. New stories arrive by the minute and remain on the system for up to a day. Enter **1** now for "US/World Headline News." A menu of stories appears, with their dates, times of arrival, and titles, as shown in Figure 11.1. Enter any item number to display the story itself, as illustrated in Figure 11.2. When you have finished the story (or pressed **M**), you will return to the stories menu. Pressing **M** a second time will return you to the NewsGrid main menu.

```
NEWSGRID (sm)  US/World Headline News
   1 08/10 1318  PRO-IRANIAN REVOLUTIONARY GROUP VOWS TO FREE U.S. ...
   2 08/10 1559  WHITE HOUSE AWAITS WORD ON HOSTAGE RELEASE
   3 08/10 1614  FORMER HOSTAGE JOHN MCCARTHY MAKES FIRST PUBLIC ...
   4 08/10 1405  JAVIER PEREZ DE CUELLAR ARRIVES IN LONDON FOR ...
   5 08/10 1604  DEADLINE TO FREE FRENCH HOSTAGE PASSES AS TROOPS ...
   6 08/10 1351  CHINA AGREES IN PRINCIPLE TO JOIN NUCLEAR ...
   7 08/10 1413  GUARDS OPEN FIRE ON DEMONSTRATORS IN MADAGASCAR, ...
   8 08/10 1239  NEARLY 20 IRAQI SOLDIERS REPORTEDLY TAKEN PRISONER ...
   9 08/10 1102  NEWS AGENCY SAYS KREMLIN SENDS CUBA $1.7 BILLION ...
  10 08/10 1305  SHUTTLE ATLANTIS CREW WRAPS UP MISSION, PREPARES ...

Enter choice !6_



  Alt-Z for Help | ANSI-BBS | 2400-E71 IDX | Cap | | |          Online 00:01
```

Figure 11.1: NewsGrid headline news

```
NEWSGRID (sm)  US/World Headline News

Ø8/1Ø 1351  CHINA AGREES IN PRINCIPLE TO JOIN NUCLEAR ...

BEIJING (AUG. 1Ø) UPI -  China, in an apparent bid to deflect Western  criticism
by showing global responsibility, has agreed in principle to join the Nuclear
Non-Proliferation Treaty, Premier Li Peng announced Saturday during talks with
Japan's prime minister.
     But Li, meeting with visiting Japanese Prime Minister Toshiki Kaifu, declined
to commit China to proposals by the leading industrial democracies designed to
better control the sales of conventional weapons to Third World nations.
     The announcement was nonetheless certain to be welcomed by Western nations,
including the United States, which in recent months has been pressing Beijing to
sign the NPT, the major international treaty limiting the spread of nuclear
weapons technology.
     Kaifu arrived earlier Saturday as the first leader of a major industrial
nation to visit China since the 1989 Tiananmen Square crackdown, bringing the
promise of expanded economic cooperation and revived prestige to China's
hard-line communist government.
     Li's unexpected announcement appeared designed to move the focus of the visit
away from human rights or other issues on which China has been criticized, and
further Beijing's recent attempts to show a more responsible image in global

Press <CR> for more !
Alt / for Help | ANSI-BBS | 24ØØ-E71 FDX | Cap |          |         Online ØØ:Ø1
```

Figure 11.2: A story on NewsGrid

Getting Market Updates

To get a market update, enter **4** from the main menu and then enter the number of an exchange or market from this menu:

```
Market Update
 1 NYSE
 2 AMEX
 3 OTC
 4 Bonds
 5 Currency
 6 Commodities
 7 Economy
Enter choice ! _
```

For instance, enter **1** for a New York Stock Exchange update and then enter **2** for "NYSE Hourly Prices," which will then be displayed, as shown in Figure 11.3.

Press **M** until you return to the NewsGrid main menu.

```
NEWSGRID (sm)  NYSE Market Update

09/13 1756  FRIDAY'S NYSE INDEXES - CLOSE

NEW YORK (SEPT. 13) UPI -  New York Stock Exchange closing indexes:
                  High     Low    Close  Net Chg.
    Composite    212.60   210.58  210.58 off 1.84
    Industrial   266.37   263.61  263.61 off 2.65
    Transport    178.27   176.97  177.56 up  0.26
    Utility       93.64    93.02   93.10 off 0.54
    Finance      157.50   156.06  156.06 off 0.86
    Equivalent to a loss of 30 cents in the average price of a N.Y.S.E. common
share.
    Volume 167,960,000 shares.

Last page !_



 Alt-Z for Help | ANSI-BBS |  2400-E71 FDX  |          |          | Online 00:01
```

Figure 11.3: NYSE market prices

Searching by Keyword

Stories remain on NewsGrid for one week. NewsGrid files stories
according to common keywords, such as names of political leaders,
countries, subjects, or the stock exchange ticker symbol. To search
for stories this way, enter **5** from the main menu, and then enter your
keyword. For instance, enter **warming** to search for stories on
global warming. At the time of this writing, this keyword turned up
one story with the heading:

**1 08/06 1859 WARMING TREND IN CHESAPEAKE BAY
COULD AGGRAVATE...**

To read a story, enter its item number. When returned to the "Enter
Keyword" prompt, press Enter to return to the main menu and then
enter **M** to leave NewsGrid.

Using AP Online

The Associated Press Online is even simpler to use than NewsGrid.
To reach the service, enter **3** from the news menu (or enter **go
apv-1** from any command prompt). News summaries are available
here through a two-tiered menu system. For instance, enter **1** from

the main menu, shown below, for the latest news:

```
AP Online APV-1
 1 Latest News-Updated Hourly
 2 Weather
 3 Sports
 4 National
 5 Washington
 6 World
 7 Political
 8 Entertainment
 9 Business News
10 Wall Street
11 Dow Jones Average
12 Feature News
13 History
Enter choice ! _
```

Enter the number of the first menu item, which will look like

```
8 AP Top Stories At 6 p.m. EDT
```

for the current hour's stories. When you are done reading, press **M** until you return to the news master menu.

Explore the Business Wire by entering **2** from the news menu. This service functions like AP Online, but specializes in business stories. It has two levels of menus. When you are done, enter **M** until you have returned to the news master menu.

Using Online Today

Online Today is CompuServe's own service, featuring news of interest to computer professionals. To bring it up, enter **9** from the news master menu (or enter **go online** from any command prompt). Try entering **4** to bring up the main menu.

Online Today's menu structure is a more complex than those of services discussed above. Keywords are a useful way to get around in this service. To see them, enter **1** for the service guide and again for the index.

Main topics are capitalized and preceded by asterisks, while subtopics are preceded by hyphens. Each line ends in a keyword. Try entering **go olt-80** for CompuServe community news. Pick an item by entering its number and page through the text. When you are done, enter **go news** to return to the news master menu.

Using the Executive News Service

This service is not available to all subscribers; to use it, you must activate the Executive Service Option as described in Step 1, which entails additional monthly charges and an extra connect surcharge of $15 dollars an hour. You get access to news services not available elsewhere, as well as to methods for filtering stories and tracking subjects of interest. You might want to read this section before deciding whether to pay for the service.

Enter **1** from the news master menu (or enter **go ens** from any command prompt) to bring up the main menu, as shown here:

```
Executive News Svc.
 1 Introduction to ENS
 2 Review Current News
 3 Search by Ticker
 4 Create/Change/Delete a Personal Folder (E)
Enter choice ! _
```

From this menu, you can scan stories from all services, look for stories on a company by ticker symbol, or create a personal folder.

Reviewing Current News

Enter **2** to review current news. You will see a menu from which you can review one or more services, as shown in Figure 11.4. To choose several services, separate them with commas or designate ranges with hyphens. Enter numbers for a few services in this way.

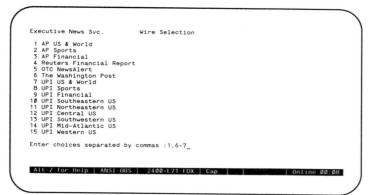

```
Executive News Svc.         Wire Selection

 1 AP US & World
 2 AP Sports
 3 AP Financial
 4 Reuters Financial Report
 5 OTC NewsAlert
 6 The Washington Post
 7 UPI US & World
 8 UPI Sports
 9 UPI Financial
10 UPI Southeastern US
11 UPI Northeastern US
12 UPI Central US
13 UPI Southwestern US
14 UPI Mid-Atlantic US
15 UPI Western US

Enter choices separated by commas :1,6-7_
```

```
Alt-/ for Help | ANSI-BBS | 2400-E71 FDX | Cap |        |        | Online 00:08
```

Figure 11.4: Choosing wire services

Executive News Svc.
 245 stories selected
 1 Scan by story titles
 2 Scan by story leads
 3 Read all stories
Enter choice ! _

You can now:

- enter **1** to see a list of story titles with sources and dates, for instance:

  1 UPn 08/10 1843 Civilian police
  employee hurt in scuffle with officers

- enter **2** to see a list of story leads, which are more complete than titles:

  1 UPn 08/10 1843 Civilian police
  employee hurt in scuffle with officers LOS
  ANGELES (UPI) -- A civilian employee of the
  Police Department was struck with a baton

> ```
> in a confrontation outside department head-
> quarters downtown with two officers, one of
> whom was also injured, authorities said
> Saturday.
> ```

- or enter **3** to page through all stories in full.

Try one of these choices. When you are done, enter **M** from the read choice menu to return to the main menu.

Searching by Ticker Symbol

You can find current news about a company by using its stock market ticker symbol. Enter **3** from the main menu and enter a symbol (such as **ibm**) from the "Ticker" prompt. You can then choose and page through selected stories. Return to the main menu when you are done.

The free NewsGrid option of searching for news by keyword may give you a more complete listing of current stories than this option.

Using a Personal Folder

A personal folder is a subdirectory that CompuServe will fill with stories on any topic you specify. Follow these steps to create a folder:

1. Enter **1** for personal folders options.

2. Enter **1** from the action menu that follows to create a personal folder.

3. Devise a name for your folder—a single word of up to ten letters that you will instantly recognize.

4. Enter a number of days for the system to save "clipped" stories in your folder (the maximum is fourteen).

5. Enter the numbers for the news services that you want searched. The menu will redisplay with your choices marked by asterisks.

6. Enter a keyphrase to identify relevant stories. For example, **global warming** would identify stories on this subject.

At this point, you may want to learn keyword syntax. If so, turn on screen capture in your communications program and enter **H** for help to see a synopsis of keyword syntax. Capture the screen, then log off and study this text.

7. Include up to six further keywords on separate lines to broaden the scope of your search.

8. Enter **4** from the action menu to list your folder and check its contents.

Your new folder will now be represented by a menu item at the main menu, such as this:

```
5 Review folder WARMING   (0 stories)
```

When you sign on and see that stories have been added, you can select this item and review the stories as you did current news stories. When you have finished reading, you will have the option of deleting stories that you have read.

This completes the news tour; sign off CompuServe as usual.

Step 12

Weather Information

CompuServe offers you a wealth of current weather information. Some reports are intended for the average commuter or recreationist, while others are directed towards serious mariners or aviators. In this step, we will examine both.

Reading Weather Reports

To bring up the weather main menu, enter **go weather** at any system prompt. Here is what the menu looks like:

```
News/Weather/Sports WEATHER
WEATHER
 1 Weather Reports
 2 Weather Maps
 3 NWS Aviation Weather
 4 Associated Press Online
Enter choice ! _
```

NWS Aviation Weather is the set of highly specialized reports for people in aviation, and Associated Press Online is another access point to the service you explored in Step 11. Therefore, we will concentrate on items 1 and 2. Enter **1** to practice reading weather reports. The subsequent menu shows the types of reports available:

```
WEATHER REPORTS
 1 (SF) Short Term Forecasts
 2 (EF) Extended Forecasts
 3 (SW) Severe Weather Alerts
 4 (PP) Precipitation Probability
 5 (SS) State Summaries
 6 (CL) Daily Climatological Reports
 7 (SP) Sports and Recreation
 8 (MF) Marine Forecasts
 9 (AW) Aviation Weather
```

```
10 (WM) Weather Maps
Enter choice! _
```

Turn on your file log to save reports of interest. If matters of interest scroll off your screen, use your communications program's scroll recall feature (in TELIX, Alt-B) to roll back to the beginning.

Choices 9 and 10 are repeated from the main menu. The remaining items are reports you can view. For instance, enter **1** to view short-term forecasts. The prompt reads:

```
SHORT TERM FORECASTS
Enter city, state,
or H for Help
SF ID: _
```

The scope of available forecasts varies from report to report, but you can always view short-term forecasts for chosen areas. Enter **san fran***—part of the city's name. (The asterisk represents the remaining characters in the name.) CompuServe responds with the report shown in Figure 12.1.

In this case, to see a specific report, enter a "meaning" in full or its corresponding ID. You can view more than one report by separating

```
SHORT TERM FORECASTS

Enter city, state,
or H for Help

SF ID: san fran*

Multiple matches for 'SAN FRAN*'

   ID        Meaning
----- -----------------------
CA002 SAN FRAN INTL ARPT   CA
SFO   SAN FRANCISCO        CA
NM010 SAN FRANCISCO PLAZA  NM

Choose ID(s), reenter location,
or <CR> to ignore: _


 Alt-Z for Help | ANSI-BBS | 2400-E71 FDX |        |        | Online 00:02
```

Figure 12.1: A local weather report

IDs with commas (for example, *ca002,sfo*). You can view reports for states by entering their two-letter postal IDs—for Arizona and New Mexico, type **az,nm**.

When you have viewed the reports, the "SF ID:" prompt reappears. You have four options here—you can

Commands at the ID prompt

1. Enter a new ID or set of IDs.

2. Enter a new report abbreviation, which you may follow with more IDs. For instance, enter **ef nat** to see an extended nationwide forecast. You will then return to an EF report prompt.

3. Enter **H** to see a summary of valid queries for this kind of report.

4. Press Enter to return to the reports menu.

Enter **help** from the reports menu and then enter a topic name to learn more about weather options. For instance, *com* shows you how to specify reports and locations, and *sports* displays a list of sites reporting conditions for sports and recreation.

Try reading a few more types of reports, noting what the initial prompt tells you about available scopes of the reports.

For a quick weather update, sign on to CompuServe and enter **weather** at any system prompt. You will be shown a weather summary for your area.

Viewing Weather Maps

You can even view weather maps online. To do so, you will need a PC with a graphics-video adapter, plus a program called OZRLE. If this does not interest you, skip ahead to the section *Viewing Weather Maps Offline*.

You can locate OZRLE by using the IBM File Finder. Download the file named OZRLE.ARC (see Step 3 for downloading procedures). OZRLE is free, except for commercial uses.

*Setting up
the online
viewer*

Unpack the constituent files from the archive (see Step 3 for tips on decompressing). Print the manual OZRLE.DOC and follow the instructions for installation. Follow your communication program's instructions to set up OZRLE as an *external file-transfer protocol*. (This is a program mode used to carry out a file transfer that a communications program is not capable of.)

*Using the
online
viewer*

To try out the viewer, sign on to your CompuServe account and enter **go weather**.

1. Press the hotkeys that you assigned to OZRLE. Following the example with TELIX, press Alt-R to receive a file and then the letter you chose to start OZRLE.

2. From the OZRLE terminal-mode screen, enter **2** to bring up the weather maps menu.

Be sure to call the maps menu from *inside* OZRLE. When this command is given, CompuServe sends a query character to see if your communications program can view files online. If your program does not respond, it will try to download the files rather than display them. Even while viewing, you can download by entering **down** *n* (where *n* is the number of a map).

3. Enter **2** to view a map of precipitation, as shown in Figure 12.2. The map files take a minute or less to transfer. When you have viewed the map, press Enter to return to the terminal-mode screen. If you want to save the weather image, enter a file name at the prompt. (The GIF extension will be added automatically.) Otherwise, just press Enter.

4. Press Home to see more options. To exit OZRLE and return to your communications program, press Alt-X.

5. Enter **R** to display an up-to-date menu. Then enter **M** to return to the weather main menu or sign off CompuServe as usual.

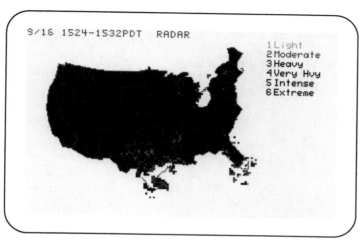

Figure 12.2: A map of precipitation

Viewing Weather Maps Offline

To view weather maps and other graphics files offline, you need a GIF viewer. You can find viewers by browsing through, for instance, the Graphics Support Forum (*go graphsupport*), library section 3. One excellent choice is a shareware program called CompuShow. It is available in the Zenith Data Systems Forum (*go zenith*), library 8, as an archive file named CSHOWA.EXE. You can write the maker at:

Canyon State Systems & Software
P.O. Box 86
Sedona, AZ 86336

CompuShow displays graphics files in many formats and with numerous options. When you register the product, you will receive an enhanced version with full instructions.

Thousands of graphics images, files, and programs are offered in the graphics forums. You reach these forums by entering *go graphics*.

Log off CompuServe now as usual.

Financial Information

A summary of CompuServe's numerous financial and investment services is beyond the scope of this book. Accordingly, this step will concentrate on their common features and show you where to look for services you need.

All financial services branch from a single menu. To begin, log on to your CompuServe account and enter **go money**. The money main menu is shown below:

```
Money Matters MONEY
1 Market Quotes/Highlights
2 Company Information
3 Brokerage Services
4 Earnings/Economic Projections
5 Micro Software Interfaces
6 Personal Finance/Insurance
7 Financial Forums
8 MicroQuote II ($)
9 Business News
10 Instructions/Fees
11 Read Before Investing
Enter choice ! _
```

One strategy for finding a service is following the most promising menu option. But take this tour to learn how to elicit information, because the menu system is complex, and a number of services entail extra charges or require the Executive Service Option.

Finding a Symbol

To get information on companies, you must supply *ticker symbols.* (These are the code names you see in a newpaper's stock market section.) To find a symbol, enter **go symbol**. The new menu, shown below, leads to symbols for bonds, indexes, and commodities, as

Ticker symbols

well as companies:

```
Money Matters SYMBOLS
ISSUE/SYMBOL LOOKUP
1 Search for Company Name,
  Ticker Symbol, or CUSIP
2 List Bonds for Company ($W)
3 Menu of Available Indexes
4 Menu of Available Commodities
5 Instructions/Fees
Enter choice ! _
```

Enter **1**. Then enter **block** at the name prompt to find the symbol for CompuServe's parent company, H & R Block, Inc. Enter **1,3**, as shown in Figure 13.1, to see all equity and debt issues (stocks, bonds, securities, and such) with *block* in the name. You will see CUSIP (Committee on Uniform Securities Identification Procedures) numbers, ticker symbols, CNUMs (four-digit codes identifying the type of issuer), single-letter exchange codes, company names, and descriptions. The ticker symbols are what we want. H & R Block, Inc. is the second listing. Its ticker symbol, therefore, is *HRB*.

```
Name: block

Name/Symbol Lookup

76 Issues found

 1 Equities (4)

 3 Debt (2)
 4 Options (70)

Enter choices or ALL !1,3

CUSIP No.  Ticker  SIC  Exc.  Issuer Name/Issue Description
---------  ------  ---- ----  ------------------------------------
09364410   BLOCA   2834  K    BLOCK DRUG INC/CLASS A
09367110   HRB     7291  N    BLOCK H & R INC/COM
09367610   BV      7822  N    BLOCKBUSTER ENTMT CORP/COM
093676AA   BV 04      0  L    BLOCKBUSTER ENTNMT CORP/LYON  00.000 04-NOV
093676AAA  BV 04      0  N    BLOCKBUSTER ENTNMT CORP/LYON  00.000 04-NOV
09368010   BLK     1382  A    BLOCKER ENERGY CORP

Last page !
 Alt-Z for Help | ANSI-BBS | 2400-E71 FDX | Cap |    |        | Online 00:01
```

Figure 13.1: Company symbols

Enter **hrb** as the ticker symbol as you practice using these services. CompuServe makes many otherwise expensive reports available free when you use this symbol.

Viewing Quotes

To get a quick market quotation, enter **go qquote** from the system prompt. There are surcharges for each quote, but you can avoid them by entering **hrb** at the "Issue:" prompt. You will be shown a quotation, aged at least fifteen minutes, giving the latest volume, high/asking and low/bid prices, and other information for the stock.

Quick quotes

At an "Issue:" prompt like this one, you can

- enter up to twenty issues, separated by commas.

- enter the beginning of a company name preceded by an asterisk (such as *block*) in place of the ticker symbol. You then must often choose a specific issue from a subsequent list.

- enter a system command by preceding it with a forward slash.

- press Enter to return to the preceding menu.

Press Enter now to return to the Market Quotes/Highlights menu, and enter **go company** to bring up the following menu:

```
Money Matters COMPANY
1 Company Analyzer ($E)
2 Value Line Data Base II
3 S&P Online ($)
4 DISCLOSURE II ($E)
5 International Company Information
6 D&B Dun's Market Identifiers
7 Business Database Plus
8 Business Dateline
```

```
9 Corporate Affiliations
10 TRW Business Credit Profiles
11 InvesText
12 Thomas Register Online
13 Instructions/Fees
Enter choice ! _
```

Enter **3** for S&P Online, a service of Standard & Poor's Corporation, then follow this sequence:

1. Enter **3** for individual company profiles.

2. Enter **1** to get reports by ticker symbol.

3. Enter **hrb** to generate a free report.

4. Enter **7** to see a balance sheet for your chosen company, that is, to display a report in this form:

```
Current Ratio 1.48
Long Term Debt .........
Shares 53.24
Report of 04/30/91
(Long Term Debt and Shares in millions)
```

Following Market Trends

Market snapshots

Market snapshots are short tables of current market trends. Enter **go snapshot** to view a snapshot similar to the one shown in Figure 13.2. The table displays current values for major market indexes as well as for the U.S. dollar. The latest updates are shown in the right column. This report requires the Executive Service Option.

Market highlights

Market highlights show the previous day's activity on the major stock exchanges. To use this service, enter **go market** and then **1**, **2**, or **3** for the New York Stock Exchange, the American Stock Exchange, or over-the-counter trading. If you enter **1**, you will see the menu that appears in Figure 13.3. Reports are grouped under "gains" and "losses." Each item includes the number of companies under

```
Current Market Snapshot SNAPSHOT

Index                        Ticker     High      Low      Last    Change   As Of
-----------------------      ------    ------    ------    ------   ------   -----
Dow Jones Industrials        DJ 3Ø    3Ø36.67   2988.6Ø  3ØØ5.37   -3.35    8/14
S&P 5ØØ Index                SP 5ØØ    391.85    389.13    389.9Ø    Ø.28    8/14
NASDAQ Composite             COMP      517.93    515.3Ø    517.68    3.28    8/14
London Gold Fix              $LGF                          355.85             8/14

Country                      Ticker   U.S. $ Equiv.   Curr. per U.S. $   As Of
-------                      ------   -------------   ----------------   -----
Yen                          XRJY        Ø.ØØ732Ø          136.61        11:16p
Deutsche Marks               XRGM        Ø.5757             1.7371       11:18p
British Pounds               XRBP        1.6867             Ø.5929       11:16p

                  Index Value          Volume (Millions)        Issues
Exchange        Latest  Change  As Of  Total   Up   Down   Advance  Decline
--------        ------  ------  -----  -----  ----  ----   -------  -------
NYSE            213.63  Ø.13%   8/14    196    1Ø8    63      887      7ØØ

Last page !
 Alt-Z for Help | ANSI-BBS | 24ØØ-E71 FDX | Cap |        |         Online ØØ:Ø3
```

Figure 13.2: A market snapshot

```
Market Highlights
                            MOST ACTIVE STOCKS
            GAINS                                  LOSSES
Updated  8/13         # of Cos      Updated  8/13         # of Cos
 1 2Ø Most Active Stocks   2Ø       11 2Ø Largest Losses       2Ø
 2 2Ø Largest Gains        2Ø       12 2Ø Largest % Losses     2Ø
 3 2Ø Largest % Gains      2Ø       13 Price Down Past 3 Days 1Ø2
 4 Price Up Past 3 Days    91       14 Price Down Past 4 Days  46
 5 Price Up Past 4 Days    35       15 Price Down Past 5 Days  16
 6 Price Up Past 5 Days    16       16 New 6-Month Low          2
 7 New 6-Month High         2       17 High Below Yesterday    55
 8 Low Above Yesterday's Hi 74      18 Volume 2X Average & Down 7Ø
 9 Volume 2X Average & Up  111      19 2Ø Largest $ Vol Losses  2Ø
1Ø 2Ø Largest $ Vol Gains  2Ø

Enter choices or ALL !_



 Alt-Z for Help | ANSI-BBS | 24ØØ-E71 FDX | Cap |        |         Online ØØ:Ø5
```

Figure 13.3: Choosing among market highlights

that report. Enter **1** to see the previous day's twenty most active stocks. You can then page through a display that includes the ticker symbol, name, volume, price, change, and percent change for each stock.

If you downloaded and configured OZRLE in Step 12, you can bring up a graph of market trends while online. (If not, skip ahead to

Graphing market trends

the section *Financial Forums*.) Follow these steps:

1. Start OZRLE (press Alt-R and then your chosen letter if you are using TELIX).

2. From the OZRLE terminal-mode screen, enter **go trend**. CompuServe will negotiate a graphics connection with OZRLE.

3. Enter **hrb** when you are prompted for an issue.

4. When prompted for an interval, enter **W** for weekly.

5. Enter a starting date in the form *MM/DD/YY,* such as 4/5/91.

6. Press Enter to accept today's date for an ending date.

7. View the graph, which should resemble Figure 13.4, and press Enter.

8. If you want to save the graph, enter a file basename (it will be given the extension GIF); otherwise, press Enter.

9. Enter **/m** when returned to the "Issue:" prompt to return to the prior menu.

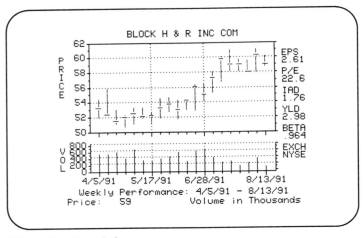

Figure 13.4: Trends for a company

10. Press Alt-X to leave OZRLE.

11. Enter **R** to refresh your communications menu.

Financial Forums

CompuServe includes several financial forums that allow you to communicate with other investors. To see a menu of these forums, enter **go finforum** from any system prompt. You can join and use any forum, as explained in Steps 5, 6, and 7.

Your Personal Finances

CompuServe places some basic number-crunching tools in your hands to help with your personal finances. To try them, enter **go fintol** from a system prompt. You can balance your checkbook, calculate your net worth, or calculate a mortgage. Enter **3** to use the mortgage calculator. Enter a hypothetical loan amount (do not use commas), such as **65000**, an interest rate, such as **8.75**, a term for the loan in years, such as **15**, and the number of payments per year, such as **12**. CompuServe will display a loan-amortization schedule like this:

```
LOAN AMORTIZATION
Loan Amount = 65000.00
APR = 8.75
Total Payments = 180.00
*******************************
Payment = 649.64
================================
Total Interest = 51935.49
Display payment schedule (W)?
(Yes or No)! _
```

Calculating a mortgage

Answer **Y** to display a payment schedule.

Page through the list of successive payments. Then log off CompuServe as usual.

Step 14

Reference Information

CompuServe is a gateway to many databases. Most are accessible through IQuest, CompuServe's main research and reference service, meaning you don't have to learn a lot of arcane database-query languages. Searches on IQuest are costly, though, so this step will first explore two less expensive services. To begin, sign on to your CompuServe account as usual.

Using Consumer Reports

The Consumer Reports service brings you five years of *Consumer Reports* magazine articles free of additional charges. The articles cover everything from automobiles to major appliances. This example will find evaluations of a recent-model car.

Enter **go consumer**. Here is the Consumer Reports main menu:

```
Consumer Reports CSR-1
CONSUMER REPORTS
All Consumer Reports materials are
(c) copyright 1986-1991 Consumers Union of US,
Inc. All rights reserved.
1 How to Use Consumer Reports
2 Appliances
3 Automobiles
4 Electronics/Cameras
5 Home
6 Index to Consumer Reports Articles
7 What's New on Consumer Reports
8 About Consumers Union
Enter choice ! _
```

It is a good idea to study the instructions before using a database. Turn on your log and enter **scroll 1** (or **s 1**). The automobile section has its own instructions, so enter **3** for automobiles and then **s 1** again. Then turn off the log. If you want a fuller understanding of the database, sign off, print and study the instructions, and then sign on again.

Finding a car model

Enter **2** to begin an automobile search. The following menu offers a choice of search criteria:

```
Consumer Reports CNS-1
Select Cars By
1 Model Year
2 Make/Manufacturer
3 Size/Type
4 Reliability
5 Recommended by Consumers Union
6 Gas Mileage
7 Model
Enter choice ! _
```

Enter **2** to search by make. Scroll through the screens until you find the desired make of car and enter its item number. For instance, choose Toyota, item *36* as of this writing. The service will report something like

```
35 Car(s) Found
```

and display a further action menu:

```
Consumer Reports CNS-20
NEXT ACTION
1 Display Car List
2 Narrow Search
3 Broaden Search
4 Undo Last Search Step
5 Start a New Search
6 Exit Automobile Search
Enter choice ! _
```

If your search discloses a lot of matching items, narrow the search by adding further criteria. This will minimize your time and connect charges. Limit your search to a given model year by entering **2** and then **1**. Then enter, for instance, **4** for 1988 (the vintage of the author's car).

If you narrow or broaden a search and then change your mind, enter **4** for "Undo Last Search Step."

When you are satisfied with your search criteria, enter **1** at the action menu to display a car list. Choose a model, and you will see a menu of reports, including *summary judgments* (capsule descriptions and evaluations), frequency of repair, and road test results. Frequency of repair shows a graph like Figure 14.1. The more stars you see, the greater the reliability.

A list of models

Using the Magazine Database

The next database on our tour is Magazine Database Plus. This service contains references and articles drawn from periodicals. As with Consumer Reports, you can navigate this service like any CompuServe area.

The Magazine Database carries some added charges ($15.00 per hour plus $1.50 for each article). To reach this service, enter **go magdb**. Capture and study the information under item 1—"What is

```
Consumer Reports      CNS-10525

FREQUENCY OF REPAIR CHART: TOYOTA TERCEL (EXCEPT WAGON)
TROUBLE SPOTS        1985    1986    1987    1988    1989    1990
Air conditioning    [*****] [*****] [*     ][***   ][***   ][***   ]
Body ext. (paint)   [******][******][****  ][***   ][***   ][***   ]
Body exterior (rust)[****  ][******][****  ][****  ][****  ][***   ]
Body hardware       [******][******][****  ][******][****  ][****  ]
Body integrity      [******][****  ][****  ][****  ][***   ][****  ]
Brakes              [******][***   ][****  ][****  ][***   ][****  ]
Clutch              [******][*****][****  ][***   ][****  ][***   ]
Driveline           [***   ][*****][****  ][****  ][***   ][****  ]
Elec. sys. (chassis)[******][*****][******][*****][****  ][***   ]
Engine cooling      [*****][****  ][***   ][****  ][***   ][****  ]

Press <CR> for more !_



 Alt-Z for Help | ANSI-BBS |  2400-E71 FDX | Cap |        |  Online 01:01
```

Figure 14.1: Frequency of repair

Magazine Database Plus?", item 2—instructions, and item 3—pricing. When you are ready, enter **7** to invoke the service. The added connect surcharge begins at this point.

Beginning a magazine search

At the opening menu, enter **1** to search the database. Enter **1** again to search by keyword. Enter the subject of some current interest, for instance, **global warming or greenhouse effect**. This search disclosed 122 matching articles at the time of writing and is succeeded by this action menu:

```
1 Display a Menu of Matching Articles
2 Narrow the Search
3 Replace (Erase) an Existing Search Method
4 Widen the Search Using an Existing Search
  Method
5 Start Over
6 Display Connect and Retrieval Charges
Enter choice ! _
```

It would take time to browse 122 article citations, so enter **2** to narrow your search. Then enter **5** to confine your search to a range of dates. The following prompt asks you to specify a range:

```
Narrowing the Search. Enter publication date
(YYMMDD) or range
(<CR> no change, ? for help): _
```

Enter **?** for more guidance and examples; the expression *910100-911030* will find articles published from January 1991 through October 1991. Once you have defined the search criteria, enter **1** from the action menu to display matching articles. Scroll through the numbered citations of these articles, as shown in Figure 14.2. When you see an interesting citation, turn on your log feature and capture it by entering **s** *n,* where *n* is the item number. The article will scroll past. This will cost you $1.50. Alternatively, you can enter **down** *n* and download the article using a protocol. When you are done, exit the database by typing **exit**. The service will list any charges you have incurred.

```
Magazine Database Plus                                 Article Citations

   19  How increasing CO2 and climate change affect forests.,
       BioScience, Sept 1990 v40 n8 p575(13).
       Article # 08884644      -- Full Text (73913 characters) --

   20  Holding back the sea. (consequences of global warming) (includes
       related article on sea-level forecast), The Futurist, Sept-Oct
       1990 v24 n5 p20(8).
       Article # 09335295      -- Full Text (25985 characters) --

   21  Paying for greenhouse research: a grant-givers' guide to the
       priorities. (editorial), The Economist, August 18, 1990 v316
       n7668 p13(1).
       Article # 09334541      -- Full Text (3831 characters) --

   22  Skiing in a greenhouse. (Science and Technology), The Economist,
       August 18, 1990 v316 n7668 p70(2).
       Article # 09334657      -- Full Text (5723 characters) --

Enter as many as 50 choices (<CR> for more, ? for help) ! scroll 19
 Alt-Z for Help │ ANSI-BBS │ 2400-E71 FDX │ Cap │        │      │Online 01:06
```

Figure 14.2: Choosing an article

There are similar databases covering other topics: Computer Database Plus (**go compdb**) for computer topics, Health Database Plus (**go hltdb**) for health issues, and Business Database Plus (**go busdb**) for business topics. To see a list of databases, type **go reference**.

Using IQuest

IQuest is an expensive service, charging by the search. To avoid the added expense of online experimentation, read through this section and apply the concepts when you make a search in earnest.

IQuest accesses databases by subject area or by name. It will also search selected databases for a given topic. The results of your search will be bibliographical references, abstracts, or full articles.

When specifying a keyword, you do not need to type the whole word. Just type the first few letters and a slash (/) as in *warm/*.

To reach IQuest, enter **go iquest** from a system prompt. Capture and study the introductory items (1 through 3). To enter the service proper, enter **4**. The main menu and prompt look like this:

```
PRESS TO SELECT * Main Menu *
1 IQuest-I System helps select the database
```

```
2 IQuest-II Search a database of your choice
3 SmartSCAN Search multiple databases
4 Instructions
5 NEW! This Month: OmniNews; Database Updates
H for Help, C for Commands
Total charges thus far: $0.00
-> _
```

IQuest commands are sometimes different from CompuServe's. Enter **C** for a brief command summary. Note the commands preceded by a slash, which control scrolling. Enter one of the paging commands (**/crt**, **/video**, or **/vt100**) to view menus and references onscreen. The print command (**/print**) scrolls articles that you can capture to your log file. Commands like this must be entered by themselves at a "->" prompt. The initial screen setting will suffice.

Enter **L** at a prompt to log off the system. Enter Ctrl-C and respond to the prompt when you must interrupt a process and return to an earlier menu.

You can read or capture further instructions for IQuest by entering **4** and making selections from the following menu. Then enter **M** to return to this main menu.

Finding References

These steps find a series of article references. This will cost $9.00 for ten references:

1. Enter **1** for IQuest-I.

2. From the menu of subject areas, enter **2** for science and technology to pursue the topic of the day, global warming.

3. The next menu consists of sub-areas of science and technology. Enter **5** to choose earth sciences.

4. The next menu offers these choices:

```
1 Search a database
2 Scan group of databases
```

```
H for Help, Co for Commands
Total charges thus far: $0.00
->  _
```

Enter **1** to search a database.

5. A menu of publication types (research journals, magazines, newsletters, books, and encyclopedias) follows. Each choice leads to a separate database. Enter **2** to choose popular magazines.

6. At the next menu, the search branches to the three forms of report that you can retrieve:

```
1 References
2 Abstracts
3 Full text
H for Help, C for Commands
Total charges thus far: $0.00
->  _
```

Enter **1** to search for references. This leads you to a database called "Magazine Database Plus."

7. Enter **1** to search by subject words (as opposed to title words, personal names, or other criteria).

8. When prompted, enter **global warming or greenhouse effect**.

9. You may now narrow your search or begin it. In practice, you should add further search criteria to limit the number of matching items. For this exercise, however, proceed with the search. First, turn on your log feature (Alt-L + *filename* when using TELIX). Enter the command **/print** if you do not want to view the references as they are captured. When the menu reappears, enter **2** to begin the search.

10. Page through the ten most recent matching references or scroll and capture them. A reference from this database is shown in Figure 14.3.

11. After the references are displayed, you will be given these choices:

```
1 Review results again
3 Order reprints
4 See additional headings
5 Start a new search
6 Leave System
Total charges thus far: $9.00
-> _
```

Enter **5** and then **2** at the following menu to return to the main menu. There, enter **/crt** or **/vt100** to return to page mode.

Finding Abstracts

Repeat the previous exercise, but choose "Abstracts" at step 6. You will bring up a database called "Readers' Guide Abstracts." Enter subject words as you did above. After narrowing your search, you will be shown ten brief headings. A menu like the one in step 11 above will offer the additional option, "See abstracts." Enter **2** to see one or more abstracts. Then turn on your log feature, enter **/print**, enter the abstract number or numbers (for instance, **1, 3, 5-8**), and

```
Heading # 5

TI Economic models and policy making on global warming.
   (environmental-economic computer simulation).
AU Miller-Alan.
SO Environment (ENVTA), volume 33, issue n6, July-August, 1991, p3(5)
PD 910700.

Press (return) to continue...->


Heading # 6

TI The Greenhouse Effect.: (book reviews).
AU Silverstein-Meryl.
SO School Library Journal (SCLJB), volume 37, issue n8, August, 1991,
   p189(1)
PD 910800.

Press (return) to continue...->
Alt-Z for Help | ANSI-BBS | 2400-E71 FDX |       |     |        | Online 00:04
```

Figure 14.3: A reference from Magazine Database Plus

confirm that you want to continue. Each abstract costs $2.00 to view and consists of about ten lines of information about the article. When you are finished, return to the main menu as before.

Reading the Text of Articles

If you repeat the previous exercise, but choose "Full text" at step 6, you will have the option of seeing the full text of the articles. Enter **2**, turn on your log feature, enter /**print**, and enter one or more item numbers. When retrieving full text, you can view one article at no charge. When it has scrolled past, return to the main menu.

Choosing a Database

To choose a database for a search, you must know the names of available databases. You can learn them by following these steps, which are free of charges:

1. From the main menu, enter **4** for instructions.

2. Turn on your logging feature and enter **2** for the database directory.

3. One way to find names of databases is through their host systems. The first page of this directory shows the host systems (such as *BRS* and *DIALOG*). We will examine them shortly.

4. Press Enter to see four screens of subject categories, including the arts, business, the States of the Union, and more.

5. You will then return to the main menu. Turn off your log. Enter **dir dialog** to see databases from DIALOG. A few are shown here (the numbers are *accession numbers,* which you can use in place of the names):

   ```
   1102 A-V ONLINE
   2848 ACADEMIC INDEX
   2099 AGRIBUSINESS U.S.A.
   2098 AGRIS INTERNATIONAL
   ```

```
1101 AIR POLLUTION TECHNICAL INFORMATION
CENTER
1095 AMERICA: HISTORY AND LIFE
1377 AMERICAN BANKER FULLTEXT
1068 AMERICAN MEN AND WOMEN OF SCIENCE
1001 AMERICAN STATISTICS INDEX
1630 API ENERGY BUSINESS NEWS INDEX
1009 AQUACULTURE
1100 AQUATIC SCIENCES AND FISHERIES
ABSTRACTS
2769 ARAB INFORMATION BANK
2519 ARCHITECTURE DATABASE
Press (return) to continue...-> _
```

Press Enter to page through this list. When you have seen enough, press Ctrl-C to return to the main menu.

6. Try finding a database by subject by entering **dir arizona**. Page through the database summaries representing two Arizona newspapers: ARIZONA REPUBLIC and PHOENIX GAZETTE. These are shorthand expressions for collections of databases. As you will learn, summary forms vary from database to database.

Searching
the
database

Let's practice searching a database; we will stop before incurring additional charges:

1. Enter **2** from the main menu to choose IQuest-II.

2. Enter **arizona republic**.

3. You will see a list of actual database names, including those covering the *Arizona Republic* since 1986. Enter **8** to choose ARIZONA REPUBLIC 1991.

4. You can search:

```
1 by subject words
2 by author name
3 by newspaper section
4 by publication date
```

```
H for Help, C for Commands
Total charges thus far: $9.00
-> _
```

Enter **M** to return to the main menu. If you were to continue the search, it would be similar to an IQuest-I search.

Scanning Databases by Topic

IQuest will scan preselected databases for topics that you specify.
To see a list of topics, turn on your logging feature and enter **scan
list** from the main menu prompt. Page through the entries and turn
off the logging feature when you return to the main menu.

To scan databases, you can

*Three ways
to scan*

- choose the scan option in the course of an IQuest-I search.

- enter **3** from the main menu and provide a subject when
  prompted.

- use the *scan* command from the main menu.

Here is a simple example using the *scan* command. If you follow it
through, it will cost $5.00 in surcharges:

1. Enter **scan anthropology** at the main menu prompt.

2. Take a hint from the search examples and enter **new
   guinea and kinship** when prompted for a subject. Enter **Y**
   to confirm that your expression is correct.

3. IQuest will indicate that it is searching appropriate databases. When this search is completed, you will see a menu
   similar to Figure 14.4. To pursue your search, enter the
   number for one of the databases shown. To avoid charges
   beyond $5.00, however, enter **M** to return to the main menu.

To exit IQuest, enter **L** from a prompt. When you return to the
IQU-1 menu, log off CompuServe as usual by entering **bye** at the
system prompt and then again at the host-name prompt.

*Leaving
IQuest*

```
Archaeology, Anthropology scan results for:  NEW GUINEA AND KINSHIP

PRESS    TO SEARCH                        Results   Format      Source Type

         Arts & Humanities Search             0     reference   journals
  1      Books in Print....................3        reference   books
         Magazine Index                       0     reference   magazines
         National Newspaper Index             0     reference   newspapers
  2      Dissertation Abstracts Online......12      abstract    dissertations
  3      Social SciSearch...................13      reference   journals
  4      Sociological Abstracts.............37      abstract    journals
  H      Database descriptions
  M      Main Menu
 SOS     Online assistance

Total charges thus far:     $5.00
-> _
```

```
 Alt-Z for Help │ ANSI-BBS │ 2400-E71 FDX │     │     │         Online 00:04
```

Figure 14.4: Results of a scan

The Official Airline Guide

The Official Airline Guide (OAG) is a comprehensive source of travel information, airline schedules, and reservations. This step will introduce you to OAG, including the all-important Electronic Edition, a flight information and reservation service.

Because OAG is independent of CompuServe, it responds to different commands. They are not difficult to learn, though. Enter **go oag** after logging on to CompuServe to reach the OAG entry menu.

You may want to read or capture the description and command summary available from this menu. Or you can call the OAG Help Desk for a printed summary of OAG commands and abbreviations. This includes codes for airports, airlines, aircraft, fares, and more. The number to call is (800) 323-4000 (outside the U.S., call (708) 562-4455).

To bring up the OAG proper, enter **5** from the entry menu. At this point, you begin incurring additional charges of $28.00 per hour days and $10.00 per hour evenings.

Navigating OAG Services

The main selection menu, shown in Figure 15.1, branches to the Electronic Edition and other OAG services. Look at some of these other services to form an idea of their scope.

The OAG prompt is a left-pointing wedge. Your communications program may not display this character; TELIX, for instance, does not. From this prompt, you enter item numbers or system commands just like in CompuServe. OAG system commands differ from CompuServe commands in that they begin with a forward slash (/). We will also run across some special commands.

```
WELCOME TO THE OAG ELECTRONIC EDITION (R) TRAVEL SERVICE - COPYRIGHT 1991
-------------------------------------------------------------------------
 1 OAG ELECTRONIC EDITION (R) - Flight Information & Reservations
 2 Airport Arrivals, Departures & Gate Information
 3 Weather
 4 Lodging & Dining
 5 Worldwide Travel Facts
 6 Travel Industry News
 7 Frequent Traveler Programs
 8 Leisure & Discount Travel
 9 Cruises
10 What's New?
11 General & How-to-Use
12 User Comments & Suggestions

        Access Nationwide Intelligence, /TO NWI, for a list of
           the 10 Best Hotels and Restaurants within a city !!!
    Need the Hotel, Resort & Conference Guide? Enter  /TO FUN  or  /TO REST!
       Enter  /I  then select item #7 for OAG Help Desk Telephone Numbers
-------------------------------------------------------------------------
Enter a number, a /TO command, or                          OFF = EXIT
X# for summary of contents (e.g., X1)
```
`Alt-Z for Help  |  ANSI-BBS  |  2400-E71 FDX  |  Cap  |        |        |  Online 00:03`

Figure 15.1: The OAG main menu

Worldwide Travel Facts

Enter **x 5** from the main menu. (The *x* specifies *expanded view*.) You will see the Worldwide Travel Facts submenu. Items include:

    World Travel Guide......................**/TO WTG**

and

    Currency Exchange Rates..................**/TO CUR**

The access command */to* is equivalent to CompuServe's *go* command; for instance, you can jump to the currency-exchange rates screen by entering */to cur* at any system prompt. Take some time now to explore this menu.

You are working here in a menu hierarchy. The bottom of the display shows command options to jump back one or more levels, such as *cm* to return to the country menu, *rm* for the regions menu, *gm* for the group menu, and *mm* for the OAG main menu.

Item 5 features extensive profiles of airlines, including on-time ratings, aircraft inventories, baggage allowances, and airports served; and airports, including location and telephone numbers, facilities, airlines represented, statistics, rental car agencies, and parking rates.

Once you have explored this branch to your satisfaction, enter **mm** to return to the main menu.

Watching Departures and Arrivals

To see the status of a given flight, you need look no farther than item 2 at the OAG main menu. (This service currently covers sixteen major U.S. airports.) Enter the item number for your airport and then for either Departures or Arrivals. You will see one or more screens of departing or arriving flights. Figure 15.2 shows United Airlines arrivals to San Francisco International Airport.

Browse the other main menu items on your own. The rest of this step will cover OAG flight information and reservations. If you want to leave the OAG at this point, enter **off** at a system prompt.

Finding Flight Information

The basic approach to using the Electronic Edition is simple and logical. Follow these steps:

1. Find available flights from your point of departure to your destination on or around the desired date and time. To

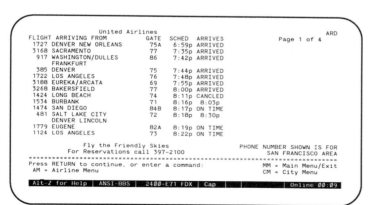

Figure 15.2: Watching flight arrivals.

broaden your choices, consider connecting flights in addition to direct ones.

2. Examine specific flights, considering exact departure and arrival times, durations, fares, meals, stops, and other such concerns.

3. Book your tickets if this service is available for your chosen airline.

Flight information changes frequently. In carrying out these steps, use the flight that actually turns up.

Finding Available Flights

You must specify airports unambiguously; this is done by using standard codes. To learn a code, you query by city name. Try finding codes for San Francisco and Paris, the points of departure and destination in our example. Enter **?san francisco**; the system will respond:

```
*RESPONSE TO YOUR HELP REQUEST*
SANFRANCISCO=
SFO-SAN FRANCISCO,CA,USA
OAK-SAN FRANCISCO,CA,USA/OAKLAND
MAKE AN ENTRY THAT WAS AVAILABLE BEFORE
YOU MADE THE SPECIFIC HELP REQUEST,
OTHERWISE ENTER /M - OAG COMMAND MENU
```

Use ? to find codes

The response tells you that the code for San Francisco International Airport is **sfo**. The "Make an Entry..." message indicates that you are still at the original menu prompt. Try entering **?paris**; you will see:

```
*RESPONSE TO YOUR HELP REQUEST*
PARIS=
PAR-PARIS,FRANCE
CDG-PARIS,FRANCE/CHARLES DE GAULLE
JPU-PARIS,FRANCE/LA DEFENSE
ORY-PARIS,FRANCE/ORLY
PRX-PARIS,TX,USA
```

as well as the "Make an Entry..." message again. Choose Orly as your hypothetical destination. (If you don't find a satisfactory flight, you can search another destination airport.)

The schedule request is initiated by the /s command. Enter /s, and OAG will prompt you for information line by line. Say that you are seeking a flight to Orly on October 10 at around 6:00 p.m. Enter:

```
/s sfo;ory;10 oct 6p
```

Direct flights from SFO to Orly are shown in Figure 15.3. Each entry represents one flight and shows departure and arrival times, destination, and other information. You can learn more about the abbreviations of airlines (*AA* or *DL*) or planes (*767*) by entering the abbreviation preceded by a question mark. Neither of the flights falls very close to 6:00 p.m., so you might want to enter *cx* to see connecting flights. Connecting-flight entries have an additional line for each hop, such as:

#	Departs	Arrives	Flight	Equip	Stops	Time
1	800A SFO	429P EWR	CO 244	AB3	0	16:15
	800P EWR	815A+1 ORY	CO 56	747	0	

```
=========================PREFERENCE STATUS:  ALL=============================
From: SAN FRANCISCO,CA,USA                        Departs: THU-10 OCTOBER, 1991
  To: PARIS,FRANCE/ORLY                                   Travel
  #     Departs         Arrives       Flight    Equip  Stops   Time
  No earlier direct flight service
  1    930A    SFO    725A+1 ORY    AA   42    767     1    13:55
  2   1215P    SFO    955A+1 ORY    DL 6180     *      1    13:40
        DL6180 757-CVG-763
  No later direct flight service
=============================================================================
ENTER A COMMAND: (#=LINE NUMBER)    A# =seats available    RS =return schedules
CX = connecting flights             B# =book flight         P =reset preferences
                                    F# =fares               ? =Help with Commands
                                    X# =expand flight



 Alt-Z for Help  | ANSI-BBS  | 2400-E71 FDX | Cap |       |            Online 00:54
```

Figure 15.3: A menu of direct flights

Here *CO* stands for Continental Airlines and *EWR* stands for New York/Newark. You can save about three hours by taking a direct flight. Return to the direct flights menu by entering **df**.

Learning More about a Flight

You can see more information about a flight by entering the expand command followed by its item number. Enter **x 1** to see more about Flight 42. You will see:

```
Expanded Direct Flight Display
Leave 9:30A On 10 OCT
From SAN FRANCISCO, CA, USA
Flight AMERICAN AIRLINES Flight 42
Aircraft BOEING 767 (ALL SERIES)
Class FIRST/COACH/ECONOMY/BUSINESS
Via CHICAGO, IL, USA/OHARE
Arrive 7:25A On 11 OCT
At PARIS, FRANCE/ORLY
Elapsed Travel Time 13 H 55 M
Enter S to return to Schedules display
Enter F to display selected fares
```

View fares for this flight by entering **F**. Figure 15.4 shows a typical fares menu. In this case, only round-trip fares appear. If a fare looks promising, enter **X** followed by the item number, to see more about it.

To make a round-trip schedule, enter **rs** from the schedules or fares menu and enter a date and time of return. Review the flight shown by entering **rs** again, then return to the original menus by pressing Enter twice.

Reserving Seats

Reserving a seat is simple, but you will not do so in this practice session. To book a seat on Flight 42, you would enter **a 1** to check seating, enter the number of seats, specify one-way or round trip, enter a return date and time, and decide on a seating class. The

```
============================================================================
Fares for AA  42 SFO/ORY
----------------------------------------------------------- Departs: THU-1Ø OCT
----------------------------------------------------------------------------
Fares: U.S. DOLLAR   *TAX NOT INCLUDED*              Fare Restriction Summary:
#  One-way    Rnd-trp    Airline/   Farecode   Cancel   Advance    Min.
   No lower fares        Class                  Penalty  Purchase   Stay   Other
1              858.ØØ      AA        HLX3ØNR  :  1ØØ%     3Ø day     7 day    *
2              918.ØØ      AA        HLW3ØNR  :  1ØØ%     3Ø day     7 day    *
3              918.ØØ      AA        VLWE     :   15%      -          -       *
4              976.ØØ      AA        HKX3ØNR  :  1ØØ%     3Ø day     7 day    *
5             1Ø36.ØØ      AA        HKW3ØNR  :  1ØØ%     3Ø day     7 day    *
6             1Ø36.ØØ      AA        VKWE     :   15%      -          -       *
7             1Ø69.ØØ      AA        MLXAP3   :  $125     21 day     7 day    *
8             1129.ØØ      AA        MLWAP3   :  $125     21 day     7 day    *
                                             * Additional Restrictions apply
============================================================================
ENTER A COMMAND: (#=line number)  L# =fare restrictions  RS =return schedules
 + = higher fares                 X# =expand fare         ?  =Help with Commands
 S = schedules                                            /Q =exit system
 -
┌─────────────────────────────────────────────────────────────────────────┐
│ Alt-Z for Help │ ANSI-BBS │ 24ØØ-E71 FDX │ Cap │     │       │Online ØØ:55│
```

Figure 15.4: A fares menu

system then asks for your name and other standard information. Cancel the reservation by entering /c and then C.

Not all airlines shown in the schedules allow automatic booking. You may have to book your flight through the airline itself or a travel agent.

Leaving the Electronic Edition

To return to the OAG main menu enter /q at a system prompt. To leave the OAG altogether, enter **off** at any system prompt. You will then return to a standard CompuServe prompt, where you can sign off as usual.

Step 16

The Personal File Area

15

The *personal file area* (PFA) is a place where you can store files on CompuServe. This is handy when you haven't got the time or disk space to download files. It is also a convenient way to transfer files from machine to machine. You can save files totalling up to 128,000 characters (192,000 with the Executive Service Option). In this step, we will examine the PFA's basic file-manipulation commands.

To begin, log on to your CompuServe account and enter **go per**.

Using the Personal File Menu

The PFA menu offers you these choices:

```
Personal File Area PER
1 Brief CATALOG of files
2 Detailed DIRECTORY of files
3 Create & edit files
4 TYPE a file's contents
5 DELETE a file
6 RENAME a file
7 COPY a file
8 Change a file's PROTECTION
9 Upload or download a file
10 PRINT a file ($)
11 Enter command mode
Enter choice ! _
```

Most of these commands have DOS equivalents. For the summary that follows, choose two short files, one text and one binary, and follow this sequence:

1. Enter **9** to initiate a file transfer.
2. Choose a file-transfer protocol; for instance, **6** for Quick B.
3. Enter **2** to choose an upload.

4. Enter **1** to transfer your ASCII text file. Of the remaining choices, *2 BINary* allows a binary transfer, and *3 IMAge* requires special software.

5. Enter a name for the file as you want it saved in the PFA, then the name of the existing file on your PC.

6. Start the local end of the transfer.

When the transfer is finished, upload the binary file:

1. Enter **2**.

2. Enter **2** for binary.

3. Enter your file names and initiate the transfer as before.

4. Enter **3** to exit to the main menu.

Try out some commands as you read their descriptions. Don't delete either file until you are done.

1. Enter **1** or **catalog** to see a brief listing of your files. This is analogous to the DOS command *dir /w*. When you have viewed the listing, press Enter to return to the menu.

As with other CompuServe menus, you can use the first three letters of the capitalized word. For instance, enter **cat** to see the file listing.

2. Enter **2** or **dir** for a more extensive listing of files, like the following:

WINBET.	3	10:11	28-Jun-91	24-Aug-91	(4)
GERI.	9	08:50	11-Jul-91	24-Aug-91	(4)
STEP5.LOG	18	20:57	24-Aug-91	24-Aug-91	(4)
DAVE.MSG	3	20:58	24-Aug-91	24-Aug-91	(4)
TEST.MSG	3	14:49	25-Aug-91	25-Aug-91	(4)

This includes the file's name, size in blocks, time and date of creation, date of last access, and protection level.

3. Enter **3** to create or edit a file. Type a message in the text editor. When you are finished, type **/exit** on a line by itself.

4. Enter **4** or **type** to show a file on the screen. This is like the DOS *type* command.

5. Enter **5** or **del** to delete a file.

6. Enter **6** or **ren** to rename a file. Use the syntax

    `ren oldname to newname`

7. Enter **7** or **copy** to make a copy of a file. Use the syntax

    `copy oldfile to newfile`

8. Enter **8** and follow the prompts to change a file's protection. Files initially have a protection level of (4), which means you can read, edit, or delete the file. Level (6), for instance, prevents you from deleting a file inadvertently. You change the protection level by entering a command in the form

    `prot filename (code)`

    where *code* is one of these digits.

9. Enter **9** to transfer a file, as you did earlier in this step.

10. Enter **10** to have CompuServe print a file and mail you a hard copy. This entails extra charges.

11. Enter **11** to enter command mode, described next.

To streamline the PFA, enter **11** to remove the menu. Then enter your commands; the system will respond *OK* to indicate it has carried them out.

You can use the PFA for e-mail messages. For instance, enter **4** from the mail main menu to *send* a message to another subscriber's PFA. Enter **2** from the mail action menu to *file* a message in the PFA.

To return the menu to the screen, enter **per**. Exit the PFA now by entering **t**, **go** *screen*, **bye**, or another navigation command.

*Using
personal
file com-
mands*

To get help on a command, enter **H** followed by the command line. Many commands have options to modify their operation. They are equivalent to what are called *switches* in DOS.

When you have familiarized yourself with the PFA, log off CompuServe as usual.

In this step, we will examine how to change your billing method, as well as explore ways to customize your log-on display.

Sign on to your account and enter **go member**. The member menu takes this form:

```
CompuServe (FREE) MEMBER
1 Change Your Billing Address
2 Change Your Billing Method
3 Change Your Password
4 Executive Service Option
5 Change Equipment/Display Profile
6 Cancel Your Membership
7 Mail Preference Service
8 Member Recommendation Program
Enter choice ! _
```

Choices 1 through 4 as well as 6 pertain to your CompuServe membership. Item 5 leads to options that control the appearance of CompuServe. The remaining items allow you to receive the monthly magazine, to place your name on a mailing list, or to recommend friends for CompuServe membership. This entire area of CompuServe is free of connect charges.

Changes to Your Membership

Your choices include changing your type of account and, for instance, where and how you are billed. Try them out now; we will bail out before actually making changes.

To change your billing address, enter **1** from the member menu. Enter **N** at the prompt to leave without actually changing your address. Enter **Y** if the information is incorrect.

Your billing address

Your billing method

Enter **2** from the member menu to change your billing method. Then enter the number of the change you want to make (credit card or bank account information; credit card or electronic funds; business account) and follow the prompts.

Your password

To change your password, enter **3** from the member menu. Enter your old password once and then your new password twice, as prompted. Turn on your communications program's local echo (in TELIX, press Alt-E) to see what you are typing.

It is good practice to change your password now and then to discourage unauthorized use of your account.

Executive Option

As you have seen, the Executive Service Option gives access to a variety of business services for a monthly premium. Enter **4** at the member menu and then either **2** to add the option or **3** to remove it.

You can cancel your CompuServe membership by entering **6** at the member menu and following the prompts.

Changing Your Display Options

Enter **5** for "Change Equipment/Display Profile" on the member menu. The master menu for changes looks like this:

```
TERMINAL/SERVICE OPTIONS (FREE)
Use this area to change your terminal type/
parameters and/or service options.
Note: Your permanent and session
settings match.
1 Instructions
2 Change permanent settings
3 Explanation of session vs. permanent
4 Show session vs. permanent
5 Change current session settings
Enter choice ! _
```

Here, choices *2* and *5* actually make the changes. Enter **2** to permanently change your account behavior. Enter **5** to make changes for the current session only. The options under the two choices are the same, except as noted. Even if you are reluctant to make permanent changes to your account, you can still experiment with your current settings and then cancel the changes. Other choices from this menu display current settings, compare current and permanent settings, or offer further explanations.

To change your session settings, enter **5** from the master settings menu, or to make permanent settings, enter **2**. Both follow roughly the same form:

```
SESSION SETTINGS
1 Explanation
2 Service options
3 Display options
4 Terminal type/parameters
5 Transfer protocol/graphic support
6 Change session settings to match
permanent
Type EXIT when done
Enter choice ! _
```

Changing Service Options

These options govern the appearance of menus and other system entities. The menu under permanent settings looks like this (the one under current settings offers only the last three options):

```
LOGON/SERVICE OPTIONS
1 First service at logon [MAIN]
2 CompuServe Mail waiting [NOTIFY ONLY]
3 Personal menu established [NO]
(Select this to create or
change a personal menu.)
4 TOP goes to [MAIN]
5 Online editor [DEFAULT]
6 Forum presentation mode [DEFAULT]
Enter choice ! _
```

Creating a personal menu

By customizing the permanent settings, you can create a menu of your favorite CompuServe services, which will appear when you first log on or whenever you enter **go top**. Make a list of services that you want to include (with their names and keywords) and follow these steps:

1. From the logon/service options menu, enter **3** to create a personal menu.

2. Enter **2** to continue.

3. Enter **1** to insert an entry.

4. Following the prompt, enter **0** because it is the first entry.

5. Specify the entry's page number or keyword (the word that follows the *go* command, such as *mail*).

6. Enter a description, such as **CompuServe Electronic Mail**, and press Enter again.

7. Repeat steps 4 through 6 for further entries, incrementing the entry numbers in step 4.

8. Enter **M** at the "Personal Menu" and again at the "Personal Menu Established" screen.

When you return to the logon/service options menu, option 1, "First service at logon," will be set to [MENU], your new menu. Enter **4** and change the target menu for the *go top* command to a page, your new menu, or to the PFA in command mode. Before leaving logon/service options, consider the remaining choices.

Choose option **2** and enter **1** if you want to go directly to e-mail when you sign on (if you have new messages).

Your online editor

When you specify option *5*, you can choose between several CompuServe editors.

Forum presentation

Option 6 governs how forums are presented. You can make settings to see menus (either short or long) or command prompts.

Changing Display Options

Enter **M** from the logon/service options menu and then enter **3**. All settings here are Yes/No toggles and are described in order:

1. *Paged display* governs whether long text displays will be paged (interrupted after each screenful) or scrolled continuously.

2. *Brief prompts* reduces system prompts to a minimum.

3. *Clear screen between pages* draws successive pages from the top of your screen, if your terminal-emulation type supports it. (See the terminal-type options below.)

4. *Blank lines sent,* if set to No, instructs CompuServe to squeeze out blank lines from its menu screens, giving you a more compressed display, useful if your terminal displays less than 24 lines.

5. *Line feeds sent.* If everything coming from CompuServe has a double-spaced effect, set this option to No and rely on your communications program to add line feeds. Alternatively, set your program *not* to add line feeds to incoming carriage returns. (In TELIX, enter Alt-O and then **T**, and then set option F, "Add line feeds after CRs," to Off.)

Making Terminal Settings

The terminal type/parameters menu tailors CompuServe to your computer terminal or to the terminal your communications program is emulating. Enter first **M** and then **4** to reach it. You have the following options:

1. *Terminal type:* Enter your terminal type, for instance "VT100" or "ANSI," from the menu.

2. *Screen width:* The standard width of a PC display is 80 columns, but you can set your account to display up to 255 columns of text if your software and hardware allow it.

Terminal settings

3. *Lines per page:* A standard PC display is 25 lines, but some software and hardware configurations allow a display of up to 50 lines. Set your account to display as many lines as your PC setup will support.

 Instead of counting your columns and lines, enter **H** after choosing item 2 or 3 to see a scale; then enter the number displayed.

4. *Form feeds:* If you use a printing terminal, set this option to Real to have your printer feed a new sheet of paper for each new page. The Simulated command tells CompuServe to send several line feeds in place of a form feed.

5. *Horizontal tabs:* Set this option to Real to have CompuServe send real ASCII Tab characters, or leave it at Simulated to substitute an appropriate number of spaces. Most communications programs respond best to spaces.

6. *Chars. received (case):* Set CompuServe to send only uppercase or only lowercase characters, if your terminal is limited in its character support.

7. *Char. sent in caps:* You can set CompuServe to display whatever you type in capital letters.

8. *Parity:* As explained in Step 1, most users set their CompuServe accounts to Even parity and 7 data bits, but you can set your parity to Zero or None and 8 data bits. You might do this if you were having problems with file transfers that involved switching from 7 bits to 8 bits and back. Some communications programs and modems can't make this switch fast enough and might even freeze. If you alter these settings, you must make the corresponding changes in your dialing-directory entry and expect signing on to be a bit cryptic.

9. *Output delays:* If your printing terminal cannot keep up with the input, add a delay between characters sent from Compu-Serve (you must determine the value experimentally).

10. *Erase when backspacing:* With this option set to Yes, the Backspace key erases as it moves. This is what most communications programs expect.

11. *Micro inquiry series at logon:* This is available as a permanent option only. If you set this option to Yes, CompuServe will send an ENQ character when you first log on. This setting is appropriate only for some specialized communications software, which will exchange a set of communications parameters with CompuServe.

You can change many Display and Terminal Type settings from any command prompt by using the *set* command with an appropriate argument. Enter **set help** to see a list of available arguments.

Setting File Transfer and Graphics Options

The final settings menu allows you to specify a default file-transfer protocol and enable graphics support. To reach this menu, enter **M** and then **5**. Then Enter **1** and the number of the file-transfer protocol you want to be the default. Or, enter **7** to see a menu of available protocols. The protocol type that you choose must be one your communications program has; you can usually edit your dialing-directory entry to make it the local default type, too.

Next, enter the number of a given form of graphics support (such as GIF) to toggle its value to Yes. This works only if your communications program offers graphics support.

If you have made changes to current session settings that you want permanent, bring up the permanent settings menu and enter **6**.

Making current settings permanent

Saving Your Settings

If you have changed your current settings, you can leave the Settings menu with current settings in effect by entering **exit**. Then use any navigation command to go to another section of the system.

If you have changed your permanent settings, you will be asked to confirm changes. Enter **1** for Yes as you leave the settings menu. Your new settings will then be saved for your future logons. Otherwise, enter 2 for No.

When you have adjusted the settings to your satisfaction, log off as usual.

Step 18
AUTOSIG

30

The three remaining steps will focus on programs designed to simplify or automate your CompuServe sessions. All of these programs are available through CompuServe and are supported by people associated with the system. In this step, we will introduce a freeware program called AUTOSIG.

AUTOSIG takes its name from *SIG,* or *Special Interest Group,* the old name for CompuServe's forums. It excels at handling forum messages: scanning headers, downloading messages automatically, and replying to messages. Messages can come from any section of a forum. AUTOSIG can also automate e-mail operations. To top things off, AUTOSIG is a complete communications program; it will perform all the text-based operations in this book.

Setting Up AUTOSIG

You may first want to study a few text files describing AUTOSIG and specifying its hardware requirements. Sign on to the IBM Communications Forum (enter **go ibmcom**), go to Library Section 1, and download the files named WHATIS.ATO and ATO*nnn*.REQ, where *nnn* is the current version number.

To secure a copy of the program itself, download the files ATO*nnn*.EXE and ATODOC.EXE. These are self-unpacking files. Create a program directory called *autosig,* log on to that directory, and run the programs. Next, print a copy of the manual, AUTOSIG.DOC. Set your printer to 60 lines-per-page if possible and enter **print autosig.doc.** The next few points summarize setting up AUTOSIG, but refer to the manual for details.

Locating program files

Setting Up Your System

Edit your CONFIG.SYS file so the "files=" line is set to 20 or higher. Also make sure your modem is set to raise its Carrier Detect line when it connects with a remote system and to pay attention to the Data Terminal Ready line.

Setting Up AUTOSIG

When you start AUTOSIG, enter your full name. You will then see the main menu, as shown in Figure 18.1.

Here is a summary of your choices:

- Press Esc to register settings for your PC (such as screen colors); press Tab to make a selection, and enter a new value for a given parameter. Press F10 to save your settings. You probably will not need to change the default values.

- Type a number key to select a Host name from the left column. For instance, *2* connects you to a CIS node at 2400 bps. Then press F4 to specify settings for the Host name. For example, type the telephone number for your local CompuServe node, press Tab, type in your user ID, press Tab again, and type in your password. The other settings should be fine for most modems and accounts, but make sure that your COM-port setting is correct, and enter your usual file-transfer path. Press F10 to save these settings.

F10 saves your changes at any settings menu, while Esc discards them.

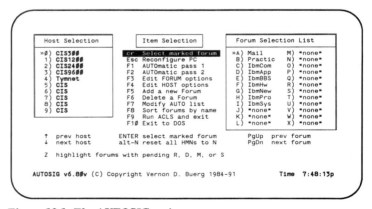

Figure 18.1: The AUTOSIG main menu

Telephone line noise can cause an automated communications program to misinterpret prompts and go out of sync with a remote service. If you see bizarre behavior or nonsense characters, redial and connect through another local node.

Setting Up Your CompuServe Account

For AUTOSIG to function properly, your CompuServe account and forums must be configured in a certain way. Fortunately, AUTOSIG takes care of much of this for you. To begin, pick the IBM Communications forum—one of the preselected forums—by typing **C** at the main menu. Press Enter to bring up the forums menu, as shown in Figure 18.2.

You can change forums from this menu by pressing PgUp or PgDn. You can return to the main menu by typing **C**. To set options, type **O**.

The following steps will configure CompuServe properly for AUTOSIG.

1. Type **G** to go online in terminal mode. *Terminal mode* is what you have used all along with your communications program. It engages the system directly. Type **Y**, and

```
Host: CIS24ØØ              Forum: IbmCom              Status: Offline

  ┌─────────────────────────────────┬─────────────────────────────────┐
  │     Online Message Processing    │     Offline Message Processing    │
  │  F  Read Forward all new messages│  R  Read and reply offline        │
  │  Q  Quick scan message headers   │  D  Download marked messages       │
  │  H  Scan Headers in message order│  M  Mark message headers for download│
  │  J  Scan headers in thread order │  P  Preview outgoing message file  │
  │  T  Read Thread all new messages │  S  Send new messages online       │
  │  U  Read CIS-marked messages only│  V  View SAVEd messages offline    │
  │  I  Read ALL messages from this ID│  W  Write new messages offline    │
  │  Y  Read ALL messages to this ID │  L  List bulletins file            │
  ├─────────────────────────────────┼─────────────────────────────────┤
  │  1  AUTO first pass   B Beeper ON/off  E  Shell for DOS commands     │
  │  2  AUTO second pass  K Delete files   O  Change forum options       │
  │  G  Go online/terminal N Update DFN file C Change forum/host         │
  │  Z  Send OFF and disconn X Exit to system ESC Change PC options      │
  └─────────────────────────────────┴─────────────────────────────────┘
  ↑↓ next host                                      «– –» next forum
                          »_«
                    Select a function

  Memory 218ØØ          HMN N          Date Ø8-31-91    Time 8:ØØ:Ø2p
```

Figure 18.2: The forums menu

AUTOSIG will log on for you. If necessary, press Esc and follow the prompts to reach terminal mode. (Terminal mode shows a status line at the bottom of the screen.) Follow the instructions in the AUTOSIG manual section "Setting Options on CompuServe: Terminal Options." These are the sort of settings that you made in Step 17. When you are done, press Ctrl-D, which gets you out of terminal mode. Type **N** at the "Stay connected?" prompt to sign off the system. Press Enter to return to the forums menu.

2. Repeat step 1 to sign on to the forum in terminal mode, but, this time, press Alt-J. This activates an AUTOSIG routine to configure the forum settings. Then, log off as before. You are now set up for AUTOSIG, CompuServe, and this particular forum.

Press Alt-A while in terminal mode to see a menu of terminal-mode options.

Working with AUTOSIG

Now that you have AUTOSIG set up, try a few of its options. The next few steps will identify interesting messages, view their contents, and draft replies. You can limit the number of sections chosen by typing **O**, entering several section numbers under Sections, and pressing F10.

1. From the forums menu, type **Q**. You will see one-line headers that show message subjects.

2. AUTOSIG will sign on, capture new message headers, and sign off. This illustrates the basic advantage of using the program—to take care of repetitive tasks and get you on and off the system quickly, minimizing connect charges. AUTOSIG captures messages above your *high message number* (HMN), that is, the last message you have viewed. If you have not been following messages on this forum, you may capture a lot of headers on your first try.

3. The next logical choice, "Mark message headers for down-load," is already highlighted—type **M** or press Enter to execute this command.

4. Scroll through the message headers. Choose messages of interest by highlighting them and typing **M** as shown in Figure 18.3. Press F10 when you are done.

5. The default option now is "Download marked messages." Either type **D** or press Enter to carry it out.

6. Once offline and back at the forums menu, type **R** or press Enter to read and reply to messages. Refer to the section "Offline Message Processing: (R) Read and reply offline" in your AUTOSIG manual for tips. Leaf through your messages by pressing PgUp and PgDn, or press **R** to bring up an editor to reply to a message.

7. If you decide to answer a message, save your reply by pressing **S**, and return to the menu by pressing F10; AUTOSIG will then send your response. You can preview your reply by typing **P**. The function keys perform various actions at the preview screen, such as cancelling the reply.

```
 Marking 'IbmCom' messages:  262 headers: HMN= 73851              162 - 184
  72953-    2:M  CompuServe & Internet?    S 5 / Ask the Sysops [C]
  73047-    1:    Shopping service          S 5 / Ask the Sysops [C]
  73049-    1:    CMU Andrew network        S 5 / Ask the Sysops [C]
  73092-    2:    Acronyms?                 S 5 / Ask the Sysops [C]
  73413-    1:    ozrle                     S 5 / Ask the Sysops [C]
  73420-    2:    Office phones             S 5 / Ask the Sysops [C]
  73476-    3:    Internet stds docs?       S 5 / Ask the Sysops [C]
  73515-    0:    X400 TMAILUK              S 5 / Ask the Sysops [C]
  73516-    0:    IBM 9370 to Dial Up PC    S 5 / Ask the Sysops [C]
  73517-    1:    FASTEST PROTOCOL?         S 5 / Ask the Sysops [C]
  73794-    0:    VOICE MAIL SOFTWARE       S 5 / Ask the Sysops [C]
  72271-    3:    Msgs to Sussex, UK        S 6 / Hot Topic [C]
  72130-   14:    9600 Modem internal?      S 7 / Modems/Comm Hdw [C]
  72288-   10:    Modem Recommendation      S 7 / Modems/Comm Hdw [C]
  72686-    0:    Low Cost 9600s            S 7 / Modems/Comm Hdw [C]
  72083-    5:    9600 Modem internal?      S 7 / Modems/Comm Hdw [C]
  72300-    1:    HAYES ULTRA 9600 Price?   S 7 / Modems/Comm Hdw [C]
  72818-    0:    Which 9600 modem?         S 7 / Modems/Comm Hdw [C]
  72835-    0:    model II to PC transfer   S 7 / Modems/Comm Hdw [C]
  72350-    2:    Gateway Troubles?         S 7 / Modems/Comm Hdw [C]
  72353-    1:    Modem switches            S 7 / Modems/Comm Hdw [C]
  72419-    1:    Need THIS voice/data sw.  S 7 / Modems/Comm Hdw [C]
  72507-    0:    Init Strg on CPQ LTE386   S 7 / Modems/Comm Hdw [C]
  M>ark     Enter = unmark    ESCape = cancel    F10 = finished
```

Figure 18.3: Quick Scan headers

Before leaving AUTOSIG, try some other options such as these, which are explained in the AUTOSIG manual:

- Download a forum-library file using terminal mode.
- Set up one or more forums for AUTOSIG and automatically scan them for messages.
- Set up CompuServe mail for AUTOSIG and check for new messages.

After logging off CompuServe, exit AUTOSIG by typing **X** from the forums menu or by pressing F10 from the main menu.

There may be times when AUTOSIG's features are too limited for your purposes. In this step, we will introduce a shareware program, TAPCIS, which offers additional features.

TAPCIS is comparable to AUTOSIG, but costs about $80 to register. For this premium, you get:

- A more sophisticated way of organizing tasks, which allows you to group together those jobs you want done online without having to write custom scripts.

- Automated access to forum libraries and files.

- A slicker menu system, with some tasks highly automated.

- An accounting module to keep track of usage and costs.

The exercises in this step are analogous to those you performed in Step 18 with AUTOSIG, to give you a basis for comparison. TAPCIS takes its name from *CIS* (an acronym for *CompuServe Information Service*).

Setting Up TAPCIS

To obtain TAPCIS, go to its support forum by typing **go tapcis**. Bring up library section 1 and download the files TAP.EXE and TAPDOC.EXE. Create and log on to a directory for the program and run these two programs. Set your printer to 62 lines-per-page and print the documentation by entering

Locating the files

```
print tapdocs.*.
```

at the DOS prompt.

What you have downloaded is a 21-day evaluation copy of TAPCIS. If you decide to keep it, register your copy as described in the manual.

*Making
settings*

Follow these steps to set up TAPCIS on your system and configure your CompuServe account for TAPCIS:

1. Set up your system and modem as for AUTOSIG.

2. Start TAPCIS by entering **tapcis** at the DOS prompt and enter your name as prompted. Type **Y** or **N** to register now or to defer registration to later.

3. The main screen appears, as shown in Figure 19.1. It is divided into online and offline tasks. Type **P** to set your communications parameters.

4. From the program parameters screen, shown in Figure 19.2, set your COM port, if necessary, by typing **C** until the correct port appears. Set these options, too: Type **T** and then **1**. Enter a CIS telephone number and a baud rate for it. Then, enter your user ID and password. Enter a path for files that TAPCIS will download. If you want to see the accounting module, type **L** until the <L>og line reads "Time and transfers." Press F7 to save your settings.

5. Press Alt-J from the main menu to have TAPCIS configure your CompuServe account to its own taste. Unlike AUTOSIG, TAPCIS adjusts these settings automatically. Also, its settings are more radical. These settings may make your account more difficult to use in terminal mode.

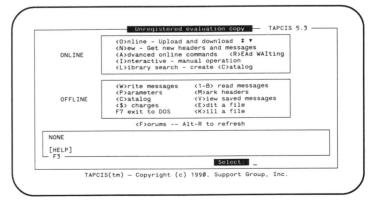

Figure 19.1: The TAPCIS main menu

```
<C>ommunications port           COM1: 8N1
<I>nitialize modem              ATV1DT
<O>nline report (4 chars.)      NECT
<F>ail report (4 chars.)        RIER
<R>eset modem                   ?3
<T>elephone numbers        <1>  555-1212              *1200
                           <2>  555-1212               1200
   Key digits 1-6 to       <3>  555-1212               1200
   change selection        <4>  555-1212               1200
   (* = selected)          <5>  555-1212               1200
                           <6>  555-1212               1200
<U>ser ID                       70000,1234
<P>assword                      [ blanked ]
<S>torage disk path
<D>ownload file path
<L>og                           None
<M>onitor colors                Norm: 7  Hi: 112  Rev: 112
<A>ppend/overwrite msg files    Overwrite
<K>eep outbox file              Never
<N>ame                          Bob Campbell
            F7 Exit or Select:  _
```

Figure 19.2: The TAPCIS parameters menu

To override TAPCIS settings, sign on to your account with your general communications program or with TAPCIS in terminal-emulation mode, enter **go member** at the opening command prompt, and configure the settings as described in Step 17.

Working with TAPCIS

As with AUTOSIG, forums must be configured to work with TAPCIS. Then, you can sign on, collect fresh message headers, mark subjects of interest, etc. Like AUTOSIG, TAPCIS has a terminal-emulation mode that lets you interact freely with CompuServe.

Unlike AUTOSIG, TAPCIS will keep you apprised of your time and expenses online.

TAPCIS keeps track of expenses!

Choosing Forums

To add forums to TAPCIS, follow this sequence:

1. Type **F** from the main menu and press F2.

2. Enter a forum name, such as **tapcis,** at the prompt. (*Appendix D* of the TAPCIS manual lists forum names.) Press Enter.

3. Enter message-section numbers separated by spaces. You can modify this list later. You must join a forum and update its settings before you can use it.

4. Specify how you want to access messages: Enter **Q** to obtain quick headers, **R** to read all messages, or **M** to read only those messages addressed to you. Repeat steps 2 through 4 for each forum you want added.

5. When you have made your selections, activate the forums by pressing their corresponding letters. An asterisk will appear in the right column. Figure 19.3 shows a selection of forums with two activated. Note that e-mail is treated as a forum.

6. Press F7 to return to the main menu, and then press Alt-J to join the selected forums. TAPCIS will take care of the details.

Selecting messages

To collect new message headers, type **N** at the main menu. This will also take you offline. Type **M** to mark headers, scroll through the list of headers, and type **R** to select messages of interest for later reading. Press F7 when you are done.

```
                                                    Press F7 to Exit
 A CIS:MAIL                             A
 B CIS:TAPCIS    Q12345                 B        * -- selected Forum
 C CIS:DATASTO   Q123                   C        ! -- unread messages
 D CIS:GRAPHSUP  Q34                    D*       ^ -- unmarked headers
 E CIS:PDP11     Q056                   E*       $ -- online action
 F                                      F        ▼ -- Library download
 G                                      G       Key:
 H                                      H        A-T toggle status
 I                                      I        F2  add
 J                                      J        F4  delete
 K                                      K        F5  move
 L                                      L        F6  swap *
 M                                      M        F8  edit options
 N                                      N        F9  select all
 O                                      O        F10 clear all
 P                                      P        Sections:
 Q                                      Q        <Ent> for CIS defaults
 R                                      R        or All, or 1 3 7 10.
 S                                      S        Q=SCA  R=REA  M=REA WAI
 T                                      T
                                                   Select:  _
```

Figure 19.3: Selecting forums

To gather the messages in their entirety, type **O** at the main menu and choose one or more forums as before. *<O>nline* is the command used to resolve any business in your in- or out-box—for instance, messages to be read or sent.

Reading messages

Go offline and read your messages from one of the forums listed in the main menu. Page through your messages by pressing PgUp and PgDn. Then, draft replies to them by typing **R**. TAPCIS will keep message headers onscreen as reminders. Return to the main menu by pressing F7 twice and send all your replies and new messages by typing **O** again.

Using Terminal Mode

Log on to CompuServe in terminal mode by pressing **I** at the main menu. Available commands are shown in the status line. If you sign off CompuServe normally while in terminal mode, you will return to the main menu.

Seeing Your Charges

TAPCIS estimates your CompuServe charges on the basis of your communications rate and other factors. To see these figures, type **$** at the main menu and press Enter. You will see a series of screens showing charges by forum and day, as well as average costs and projections. These figures are estimates, though. To see official figures, enter **go rates** while online to CompuServe.

To exit TAPCIS, press F7 from the main menu and then press any key (except F1) to confirm.

The final program we will look at is the CompuServe Information Manager, which adds a windows-based interface to CompuServe. With CIM, the ability to navigate menu choices largely replaces the need to memorize commands. The menu and command options are easy to learn, because they correspond to commands you already know.

Unlike AUTOSIG and TAPCIS, CIM is not designed to handle a lot of messages or get you logged on and off quickly. On the other hand, it helps you locate, consider, and deal with individual messages and files.

Obtaining and Installing the Information Manager

Unlike other software packages described in this book, CIM cannot be downloaded. You must order it from CompuServe. Log on as usual and enter **go cimsoft**. Order the package by choosing the appropriate menu item or by entering **go order**. The software will then be shipped to you. Although it is not shareware, it is not expensive—currently $25.00.

Before purchasing CIM, you might want to read through this step to determine whether it would be of benefit to you.

To install CIM, insert the first disk into your floppy-disk drive. Type

```
a:install
```

at the DOS prompt and follow the prompts. When the program is installed, enter **cim** at the DOS prompt and provide your name, user ID, password, and serial port. CIM will function with your normal CompuServe menu settings, so you can alternate between CIM and a standard communications program.

Working with the Information Manager

CIM presents an initial "desktop," which includes an opening menu of frequently used services, as shown in Figure 20.1. Highlight one of these choices and press Enter or click on the option with the mouse. All choices have mouse equivalents. CIM will log on to the service and go to the appropriate area. Your total connect time is displayed in the upper-right corner of the screen. Press the Alt key or F10 to activate the menu bar. You can exit any window or menu by pressing Esc.

Follow these steps to log on to a forum and check for new messages:

1. Highlight one of the choices on the opening menu and press Enter.

2. Once logged on to the forum, activate the menu bar by pressing F10. Highlight Messages with the right-arrow key and choose Browse from the pull-down menu, as shown in Figure 20.2.

3. You will see a series of message topics, with the number of threads and individual messages under each topic.

4. Choose a topic. The first message will appear along with its header and a series of command buttons. Press Message to

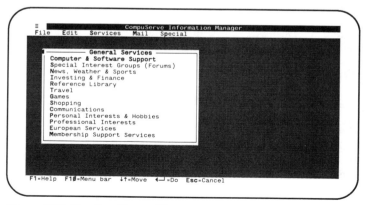

Figure 20.1: Reading Forum Messages

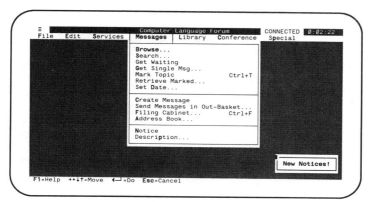

Figure 20.2: Browsing messages

advance to the next message, Topic to advance to the next thread, or File It to save the message in a "folder." Select a button by moving your pointer to it and double-clicking the mouse. If using the keyboard, press Tab or an Alt-key combination to highlight a button and press Enter.

Save your messages in a folder and formulate your replies offline. This saves connect time and, consequently, money. All three automatic-access programs described in this book offer this advantage.

The Map command button brings up a diagram of messages in the current thread, as shown in Figure 20.3. Select any message in the map to display it. Also, look at the status line at the bottom of the figure. CIM displays forum events here, such as someone changing his forum settings.

Mapping messages

Browsing Files

Without closing any windows, browse the forum files by pulling down the Library menu and selecting Browse. Select first a file section and then a particular file to see a summary of that file and a set of command buttons. The Abstract window offers a summary of contents plus a further option to view text files online. The other choices should be obvious.

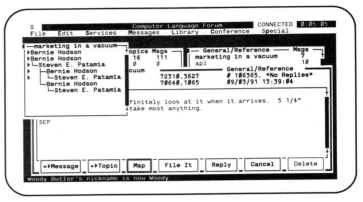

```
 ≡            Computer Language Forum        CONNECTED ▓:▓5:▓5
 File    Edit    Services    Messages    Library    Conference    Special
▌—marketing in a vacuum—┐
▐▶Bernie Hodson        ║Topics Msgs ——┐  ┌— General/Reference —— Msgs ┐
▐▶Bernie Hodson        ║   16    111 ║  ║  marketing in a vacuum      7 ║
▐▶└Steven E. Patamia    ║    ▓      ▓  ║  ║  apl                      1▓ ║
▐▶                      ║cuum          ║  ║—— General/Reference ——
▐▶  ├Bernie Hodson      ║      72310,3627 ║  ║  # 1▓6365, *No Replies*
▐▶  └Steven E. Patamia  ║      7▓64▓,1▓65 ║  ║  ▓9/▓3/91 13:39:▓4
▐   └Bernie Hodson      
▐     └Steven E. Patamia  ║finitely look at it when it arrives.  5 1/4"
                         ║take most anything.
 ┌─┐
 │ │SEP
 └─┘

 ┌─────────┐┌────────┐┌─────┐┌─────────┐┌────────┐┌────────┐┌────────┐
 │—▶Message││—▶Topic ││ Map ││ File It ││ Reply  ││ Cancel ││ Delete │
 └─────────┘└────────┘└─────┘└─────────┘└────────┘└────────┘└────────┘
 Woody Butler's nickname is now Woody
```

Figure 20.3: The message map

Because CIM works behind the scenes, windows and lists sometimes take a moment to appear (hence, the *working* message in the
upper-right corner). Also, as you scroll down a list, items will
sometimes be slow in appearing. When you hit the bottom of a list,
the program will beep.

Visiting Favorite Places

CIM's Favorite Places option (in the Services menu) is a customizable
menu of the areas in CompuServe you frequent most. For example,
Airline Reservations is already listed when you install the program.
Bring up the Official Airline Guide by following these steps:

1. Select Airline Reservations under Favorite Places.

2. Select the OAG Electronic Edition from the following
    menu. CIM will warn you of OAG surcharges.

3. If you proceed, the OAG opening menu will appear. Be-
    cause CIM does not automate the OAG, the program will
    enter terminal mode. For more information on the OAG,
    see Step 15. When you enter **off**, the CIM desktop will
    reappear.

You can switch to terminal mode at any time by selecting Terminal Emulator under the Special menu.

Handling Your Mail

CIM automates handling your mail. You send new mail simply by selecting Create Mail under the Mail menu and following the prompts. You may omit the address if you have an Address-Book entry for your recipient. You can edit your Address Book using CIM.

When you have received new mail, you will see the message "Mail!" in the lower-right corner of your screen. Simply double-click on the button to read incoming messages. You are presented with several options, as shown in Figure 20.4.

Using CIM, you log off CompuServe by pressing Ctrl-D. Do so now. Then exit the program by choosing Exit from the Files menu or by pressing Alt-X.

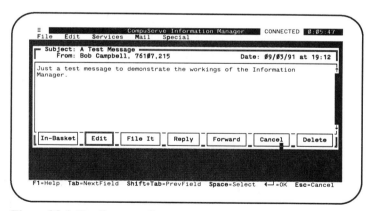

Figure 20.4: Reading e-mail

Index

! (exclamation point), 7, 9
($) menu flag, 9
% (percent sign), 43
/ (slash), 16, 40
: prompt, 16

AUTOSIG program, 119–124
  main menu for, 120
  obtaining, 119
  setting up, 119–122
  working with, 122–124

A

Address Book, 46–48
  adding entries to, 47
  adding yourself to, 48
  listing entries in, 47
agreement number, 5
Announcements forum option,
  25
AP Online, 66–67, 73
ARC files, 21, 34
archived files
  directory for, 21
  formats for, 21
  preparing, 20–22
ASCII file transfers, 1, 36–37
ASCII text files
  downloading, 24, 36
  printing, 24
  uploading, 31, 53, 108
Associated Press Online, 66–67,
  73
author's address, 47, 55
AUTOEXEC.BAT file, 21
automatic dialing, 1

B

baud rates, 3–4, 10–11
billing, 5, 111
binary files, 34
  downloading, 59
  uploading, 54, 108
bps rate. *See* baud rates
break command, 43
browsing library files, 33–35, 38

C

calculations, 85
CAT files, 34
CB Simulator, 43
charges
  communications, 3–4
  connect-time, 3–4, 10
  Executive News Service, 68
  IQuest, 91
  Magazine Database Plus, 89
  Online Tour, 6
  Practice Forum, 6

exclamation point (!), 7, 9
Executive News Service, 63,
  68–71
  adding/removing, 112
  charges for, 68
  getting market snapshots with,
    82
  personal folders in, 70–71
  searching by ticker symbol in,
    70
Executive Service Option, 3,
  9–10, 63
external file-transfer protocols, 76

F

Favorite Places option, 134–135
file transfers, 1, 5, 35–37
  ASCII text file, 36, 53, 108
  ASCII vs. protocol, 36
  binary file, 34, 54, 59, 108
  external protocols for, 76
  list of protocols for, 37
files. *See also* library files
  archived, 20–22
  ASCII text, 24, 34, 36, 108
  binary, 34, 54, 59, 108
  checking size of, 19, 34
  downloading, 18–20, 24
  filename extensions, 34
  finding, 16–18, 20
  IBM File Finder for, 16–18, 35
  personal file area (PFA),
    107–110
  storing on CompuServe, 107
  uploading, 107–108

financial forums, 85
financial services, 79–85, main
  menu for, 79
Find a Topic menu, 15–16
find command, 16, 39
forum conferences, 39–43
  getting help, 43
  identifying conference partici-
    pants, 41
  identifying forum users, 40
  interacting in, 40–43
  joining, 39
  monitoring, 42
  private, 42–43
  sending private messages, 42
  signing off, 43
forum libraries, 33–38
forum messages, 27–31
  composing, 30–31
  finding, 27–29
  reading, 28, 132–133
  replying to, 30–31
  selecting, 27–28
  selecting by age, 28
  selecting by section name,
    28–29
  selecting by subject, 29
  sending, 30–31
  size limit of, 31
  uploading, 31
  viewing, 27–28
Forum Options menu, 25–26
forums, 23. *See also* forum
  messages
  Announcements option, 25
  commands for, 23
  configuring for AUTOSIG,
    121–122

Selections from The SYBEX Library

COMMUNICATIONS

Mastering Serial Communications
Peter W. Gofton

289pp. Ref. 180-2

The software side of communications, with details on the IBM PC's serial programming, the XMODEM and Kermit protocols, non-ASCII data transfer, interrupt-level programming, and more. Sample programs in C, assembly language and BASIC.

Mastering UNIX Serial Communications
Peter W. Gofton

307pp. Ref. 708-8

The complete guide to serial communications under UNIX. Part I introduces essential concepts and techniques, while Part II explores UNIX ports, drivers, and utilities, including MAIL, UUCP, and others. Part III is for C programmers, with six in-depth chapters on communications programming under UNIX.

Understanding PROCOMM PLUS 2.0 (Second Edition)
Bob Campbell

393pp; Ref. 861-0

This in-depth tutorial on communications with PROCOMM PLUS is now updated and expanded for version 2.0. It's still the best guide to PROCOMM PLUS, showing how to choose and install hardware; conncect with on-line services and other computers; send and receive files; create and use MetaKeys and scripts; and more.

Up & Running with PROCOMM PLUS
Bob Campbell

134pp. Ref. 794-0

Get a fast-paced overview of telecommunications with PROCOMM PLUS, in just 20 steps. Each step takes only 15 minutes to an hour to complete, covering the essentials of installing and running the software, setting parameters, dialing, connecting with and using an online service, sending and receiving files, using macros and scripts, and operating a bulletin board.

Up & Running with PROCOMM PLUS 2.0
Bob Campbell

140pp; Ref. 879-3

Learn PROCOMM PLUS 2.0 (and 2.01), and gain a basic understanding of telecommunications—all in just 20 steps. Each step takes only 15 minutes to an hour to complete, covering such topics as program installation and navigation; creating and using a bulletin board; using script files to save time; using CompuServe; more.

UTILITIES

The Computer Virus Protection Handbook
Colin Haynes

192pp. Ref. 696-0

This book is the equivalent of an intensive emergency preparedness seminar on computer viruses. Readers learn what viruses are, how they are created, and how they infect systems. Step-by-step procedures help computer users to identify vulnerabilities, and to assess the consequences of a virus infection. Strategies on coping with viruses, as well as methods of data recovery, make this book well worth the investment.

Mastering the Norton Utilities 5
Peter Dyson

400pp, Ref. 725-8

This complete guide to installing and using the Norton Utilities 5 is a must for beginning and experienced users alike. It offers a clear, detailed description of each utility, with options, uses and examples—so users can quickly identify the programs they need and put Norton right to work. Includes valuable coverage of the newest Norton enhancements.